how to be her
KITCHEN
LOVE
GOD.

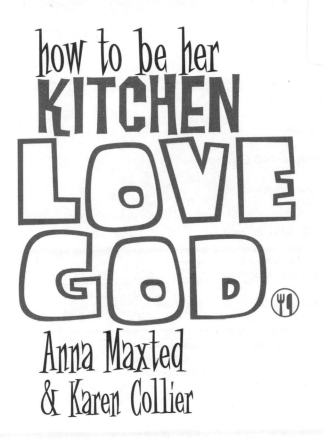

Anna Maxted
& Karen Collier

Thorsons

Thorsons
An Imprint of HarperCollins*Publishers*
77-85 Fulham Palace Road
Hammersmith, London W6 8JB

The Thorsons website address is: www.thorsons.com

Published by Thorsons in association with
Cosmopolitan magazine 2000

A catalogue record for this book is available
from the British Library

ISBN 0 7225 4037 X

Printed and bound in Great Britain by
Martins the Printers Ltd, Berwick upon Tweed

Contents

Introduction

Why this book?

Potato wedges. Tuna pasta. Mushroom stir-fry. Cheese straws. The 'fish dish'. This sorry list represents the sum total of the average young woman's culinary expertise. I know this because I've just asked my girlfriends what they can cook. This explains why we always eat out. Most women no longer have the time and/or inclination to read a recipe, let alone forage for the ingredients and put it all prettily together. Furthermore, we're still smarting from the time, aged 11, we made scones at school with lard, and our vegetarian aunt took one bite and spat the rock of our labour into the sink.

We know that cooking is, potentially, soothing and satisfying but, after a hard day at work, we don't have the energy to find out. When we eat alone, we are disgracefully lazy – far lazier than men – and often

Don't panic – you don't actually have to be a good cook to score the points – you just have to look like one, and to produce a limited number of reasonable results. Left to themselves, most men are happy and healthy with a very basic diet. Beer, rice, vegetables, chilli, and the odd chunk of meat – that's a man's diet. It isn't going to pull the babes though, so play close attention to what follows.

(Extract from *How to be a Man* by John Birmingham and Dick Flinthart)

Cooking at home is cheaper than eating out. And considerably healthier than trying to live on burgers and Mars Bars. Generations of men have learned to cook, however, for one main reason: it's a top way to impress the babes.

(Extract from *How to be a Man* by John Birmingham and Dick Flinthart)

resort to munching cereal straight from the packet. If we're in a nutritious mood, we might go mad and heat up some fast-cook spaghetti. Or, if we're feeling exceptionally flash, we'll treat ourselves and microwave a slab of cod.

When we have company, we might – if we really like you – dust off the Good Housekeeping tome our mother bought us and attempt to make you a cashew chicken. That said, if we settle for Marks & Spencer's best, it probably means we really, really like you and don't want to put you off us. It's not that we hate cooking, it's that we have other things to do that we're better at. Like staying out late. Clubbing. Networking. Reading. Talking on the phone. Washing our hair. Meeting delicious men such as you. These pastimes are fun

Cooking impresses for many reasons. In the first place, women don't expect you to be able to cook. At best, they expect to see scorched meat, boiled potatoes and soggy vegetables, in the best British tradition. A man who can rustle up a quick and elegant Thai salad, or perhaps a Cantonese crab-and-sweetcorn soup, or even a platter of rich, piquant spaghetti Bolognese – this is a surprising man, a competent man, a sensitive man who has a fast-track to the bedroom of his choice.

(Extract from *How to be a Man* by John Birmingham and Dick Flinthart)

TACTICAL ADVANTAGES OF KNOWING HOW TO RUN UP AN IMPRESSIVE MEAL

Suppose you meet The Killer Babe at work, or get to know her on the bus, or through a bunch of friends – in fact, anywhere but in the classic pickup spots of pub and nightclub, where the rules of approach are already clearly defined. You get to know her, moving slowly and carefully, and when you figure enough time has passed, you move in. What will you do? Is it going to be a film? A show? A night at the restaurant?

Passé, gentlemen. All of the above have one disadvantage: they are clearly **dates** and a man who asks a woman out on a **date** has (let's be honest with one another shall we?) only one goal. She knows it. He knows she knows it. She probably even knows he knows … and so on. Anyway, suddenly the situation has gone from 'friends in a social context' to 'sniffing each others butts'.

and rewarding – like cooking, in fact – but the truth is, fussing over a hob is not the done thing for a funky, modern, independent woman. We may as well wear a pinafore and call ourselves Margaret. Cooking is so *painfully* old-fashioned. Unless, of course, you're a man. If you're a man it's just about the best thing you can possibly do.

Cooking is such an asset! It's so now! It's so exquisitely attractive! Admittedly, it's partly attractive because we can plop ourselves onto a sofa and channel-hop while you chop, slice, dice, mince, grind, drizzle and grizzle for two hours. It's also attractive because we like to see you make the effort for us.

End result? Going on a **date** is one of the most arduous and traumatic social experiences a man can undertake outside of polar expeditions and a stint in the Foreign Legion.

The man who can cook, though – he has more options. He can, for example, suggest something far more innocuous – a trip to the football or rugby, or a day at the races together, if she happens to like that kind of thing. Or a day jaunt to the beach or maybe a drive to the country with a couple of friends to check out the local craft markets. Now **that's** not really a date, no sir. Craft markets are about as sexually non-threatening as it gets. And if our man happened to bring a picnic basket, carefully loaded with the right goodies plus one or two niftily prepared dishes … well, picnics are **romantic**, you see. Not like a date at all. Not with those other friends along. Make those specially prepared dishes really impressive, let the wine flow, and soon the non-date picnic will take on an altogether more intimate atmosphere.

(Extract from *How to be a Man*
by John Birmingham and Dick Hinthart)

Never underestimate the seductive power of making a huge, monstrous, time-consuming, exhausting effort for a woman.

Women love you when you cook. It makes them feel nurtured and important. A man who cooks is a man to be boasted about. If a man can cook, a woman assumes all kinds of flattering things about him, and so do all her friends. Smart men understand this, which is why increasing numbers of men are flash with a pan. Why not be one of them?

HOW TO BE HER KITCHEN LOVE GOD

- Vegetable Stock
- Chicken Stock
- Fish Stock
- Meat Stock
- Gravy
- Simple White Sauce
- Fresh Tomato Sauce
- Rich Chocolate Sauce
- Flavoured Butters:
  Herb Butter
  Garlic Butter

1.

GETTING
started

Here are a few hints, tips and essential items to arm yourself with before discovering your culinary skills. They will help ensure that things run as smoothly as possible in the kitchen.

Store cupboard essentials

It's a good idea to stock up on a few essentials so you don't have to search out Tesco's for every single ingredient you need when you come to cook up your recipe. A well-stocked store cupboard also means you have these items to hand to whisk up an impromptu meal or snack. Sometimes they form the basis of an entire dish, with just one or two fresh ingredients needing to be added.

Store-cupboard ingredients usually last a long time but keep a check on the use-by date. Once opened, store them in airtight containers or in the fridge, if necessary. Here is a list of handy items to stock:

Learn to shop. Find your local deli. Check out the range of fresh fruit and veg at the nearest supermarkets and compare them with the greengrocers. Find a source of organic fruit and veggies. Will the neighbourhood greengrocer get special stuff in if you request it? What days does trout turn up at the fish place? Very, very few foods benefit from extended refrigeration. Try to get what you need fresh for the day you intend to use it. Build your menu around what you can get locally that's of good quality — the same way the best chefs work their restaurants.

(Extract from *How to be a Man* by John Birmingham and Dick Flinthart)

In the cupboard

- tins of tomatoes
- tomato purée
- extra virgin olive oil
- white and red wine vinegar
- balsamic vinegar
- mustard
- tins of soup (Baxters is excellent)
- jar of pesto
- curry paste or powder (Pataks is good)
- tins of chick-peas, petit pois, cannellini, haricot and kidney beans
- tins of tuna or salmon
- soy and Worcester sauce
- Italian-made dried pasta
- rice, white or brown
- at least two dried herbs and two spices, such as thyme and oregano, cumin and coriander
- dried chillies.

In the freezer

- Parmesan cheese, grated from a whole lump and tightly sealed in a bag
- vegetables, such as sweetcorn, peas and spinach
- chopped fresh herbs.

Tools of the trade

It is essential to equip yourselves with the tools of the trade. Shiny new things boost your confidence and efficiency and

HOW TO BE HER KITCHEN LOVE GOD

enable you to whirl around the kitchen, slicing, grating, basting, whisking, liquidising, et impressive cetera without stopping and stumbling because you lack the correct equipment.

Don't get too carried away, though, and think simple. Do you really need that electric can opener, for instance, or an electric carving knife? Also, think about the amount of space you have in the kitchen.

Boys' own guide – the right stuff

Here's a list of the Absolute Minimum you *must have* in your kitchen. We have a lot more flash gear in our respective love shacks because we are complete wizards who know that hundreds of pounds spent in the kitchen pays off admirably in the boudoir. But you are a mere novice who needs to be led through a kindergarten level cookery course. Note that stove, oven, and refrigerator with a freezer compartment go without saying. A kitchen without those three is just a spare bedroom.

Bamboo steamers
Two, plus one lid (they stack on top of each other). Buy them to fit in your wok. Very useful for quickly preparing tasty vegetables, and occasionally running up Chinese-style dumplings.

Colander
Solid plastic job. Drains pasta, tosses salads, makes a great helmet in war games.

Cutting board
The super-duper toughened glass variety because it washes easily, and doesn't harbour Evil Germs. Dense plastic is next, but has a much shorter lifespan. Wood is not a good idea for

anything but vegetables and breads. Don't make us tell you what a chopping board is for.

Decent cleaver

Chinese-style tong-axes in mild steel can be bought from the larger Chinese grocers. This is your all-purpose knife. After the wok, your cleaver is your next-best mate in the kitchen – all your chopping, dicing, slicing, cutting and bone-cracking will be done with the cleaver. It's perfect for home defence too. Keep it sharp, keep it oiled, and keep it handy. If you can afford a really authoritative cleaver with a heavy spine, a wooden handle and a curved cutting edge you'll have a friend for life. It also slices pizza like a dream.

Frying pan

About 25cm across on the inside cooking surface. Cast iron – no substitutes at all. And make absolutely certain it has a wooden handle, well attached. Cast iron gets hot, and if you haven't got something to grip it with, you'll do yourself a serious injury one day. With sandpaper, remove any surface rust. Then season your frying pan exactly as you did your wok, and treat it in the same manner. Well-treated cast iron eventually becomes nearly as smooth and slick as Teflon-coated aluminium – which you must *never* waste your time with! Your frying pan is where you'll manage bacon and eggs, and pancakes, and where you'll turn out the occasional, beautifully rare steak.

Good, strong sharp kitchen scissors

After the cleaver, these are your next-best friend in the kitchen. They are just the absolute best things for preparing meat for stir-fries, clipping bits off things, trimming fat, and a dozen other operations.

HOW TO BE HER KITCHEN LOVE GOD

Ladle

It's really hard to serve soups and sauces without this.

Large saucepan/stock-pot (5-10 litre capacity)

Stainless steel. No substitutes. This is where you'll make your soups and stocks, bulk pasta, and extra large portions of chilli con carni or Bolognaise sauce.

Long, serrated bread knife

Just a cheap one will do. You need this for slicing bread and carving the occasional roast.

Measuring jug

Just the one will do, but it should be graded both metric and imperial, and should show cup measurements as well. Pyrex glass or dense, transparent, heat resistant plastic.

Medium saucepan (about 2-3 litre capacity)

Stainless steel, or at worst (and it really is worst) enamelled metal. Make sure the lid fits well and has a steam vent, and that the handle is sound and well attached. Medium saucepans are where your pasta and sauces get done. Small saucepans are cute, but they're a pain in the arse, and anything you can do in one of them, you can do in a medium saucepan.

Miscellaneous kitchen drawer stuff

Two pairs of stainless steel salad tongs, a good can-opener and a corkscrew.

Mixing bowls

At least three, of 4–5 litres capacity each. Spun stainless steel is best. You need these for holding ingredients, mixing batters, and whipping cream.

Pyrex casserole dish with lid
Get the right size for making pies as well as small casseroles and two-person lasagne. Be absolutely certain it's Pyrex.

Rice cooker
Even a moron could use one.

Roasting pans
Two of them, about 10cm deep, and maybe 40cm x 25cm in size. Go for stainless steel. These are for roasting and baking.

Rolling pin
Wooden ones are cheaper but a marble or granite job from a kitchen shop will make your life a lot easier. An absolute necessity for pastries and pizza crusts.

Salad bowls
Two, large wood-laminate bowls. These are for serving salads of all kinds, and nothing else. Find another container for your stash.

Sealable Tupperware® bowls
At least three, of 3–5 litres capacity each. Vital for storing leftovers in the refrigerator.

Short, sharp knife
About the size of a paring knife, perhaps a little longer. You need this for fiddly cutting jobs.

Spatula
Stainless steel, with a dense plastic handle. Used for dealing with hot stuff on your frying pan, like pancakes and omelettes.

Whisk
Solid handle, preferably stainless steel. Don't get the kind with the wrapped-wire spring handles. They rust out from the inside.

You need it for working with sauces, whipping cream, and most importantly for beating eggs.

Wok: carbon steel, flat-based
Get one with a nice big wooden handle, and a well fitted lid. Season it before use by washing it, then slowly heating it with a thick layer of peanut oil. After that you should never soap it again – wash it with an abrasive pad and hot water, and wipe another fine layer of peanut oil on it after each use. Your wok is your best buddy in the kitchen; you can stir-fry, deep-fry, and steam with it. At a pinch, you can even use it for Western-style cooking.

Wooden spoons
At least three, with fairly long handles. These are for stirring rich sauces and heavy batters as you cook, and for tossing stir-fry.

This list is an absolute minimum for absolute beginners. Don't cut anything out of it. Don't start inviting potential victims over for dinner until you've got it all, learned to use it, and put everything on the list away in a place where you can always find it again. If you've done all that, though, and you find yourself liking this habit of cooking, you should consider getting a few more items which, while not absolutely essential, will make your life in the kitchen a lot easier and more fun.

Extra items for the pro-kitchen cupboard
Basting/pastry brush
Basting spoon
Cake and bread tins
Can opener
Cheese grater

Citrus press and zester

Electric mixer (whips cream and beats eggs really quickly)

Fish slice

Flat baking sheets (for biscuits!)

Fondue set (enormous fun)

Food processor (they're brilliant, but the cheap ones fall apart within three months)

Frying pans and lids

Garlic press

Ice-cream scoop

Kitchen scales

Kitchen scissors and tongs

Knife sharpener

Microwave oven (for defrosting and reheating only. The one exception is for melting Mars Bars and we never do this unless we know the young lady very well. Do we, gentlemen?)

Oven mitts

Pestle and mortar (granite. For grinding spice pastes)

Piping bag (hard to fill profiteroles without it – and ho, how women adore a good profiterole in the bed, heh-heh-heh)

Portable gas ring and bottle (cooking on electricity sucks. A mobile gas ring is fantastic, especially for picnics, but also for cooking at the table.

Potato peeler

Weird metal-mesh ladle (for getting things into and out of really hot fat)

Wire cooling rack

Wooden spoon

HOW TO BE HER KITCHEN LOVE GOD

Cooking tips and advice

When deciding on what to cook, whether just for the two of you or for a dinner party, the golden rule is to steer clear of a meal that you find too complicated or unfamiliar. Instead, choose something that you feel confident about, to avoid kitchen tantrums and traumas.

Planning a menu

Make the menu as well-balanced as possible. Think about the mix of flavours, textures and colours – rich and light, sweet and savoury, crunchy and smooth, hot and cold. Try to avoid duplicating ingredients, such as serving cream in every course, or featuring fruit in every dish.

Where possible, choose a recipe that uses fresh produce in season. It will be at its peak for flavour and best value for money.

Always check whether any of your guests are vegetarian or have special dietary needs or allergies.

Buy all of your ingredients in advance, especially exotic or unusual ones. That way, you save yourself from a last-minute panic rush to the corner shop where you'll be lucky to find a tin of prunes, let alone fresh figs.

It may seem obvious, but make sure you carefully read the recipe well before you start. For instance, you don't want to be cooking away, only to make the nasty discovery that a meal you plan to serve in half an hour entails marinating the meat for three hours.

Weigh out the ingredients beforehand and prepare them too – it will usually tell you in the list if your carrots need to be diced or your mushrooms sliced – so that you have more time when it comes to the actual cooking. Recipes will also often tell you if anything can be cooked in advance. Take advantage of this, especially if you have been crazy enough to volunteer to cook a ritzy three-course affair for 10.

Be prepared. The most important thing about cooking for sex is that it should never look like a gigantic struggle. The ideal meal is one which looks and tastes impressive, but doesn't really require that much effort. You don't want to be exhausted after you've done all that groundwork, do you?

(Extract from *How to be a Man* by John Birmingham and Dick Flinthart)

A dinner which consists entirely of rich, meaty dishes may taste great, but nobody is going to be able to finish it and you can forget about the bedroom gymnastics afterwards. Remember your nice, healthy food-group balance: go for a good proportion of grains to vegetables to meats, and when you're trying to impress, don't be afraid to step just a little onto the naughty-but-tasty side of the ledger. Likewise, keep the servings reasonably small as you don't want to find that the evening ends with everyone lying around, clutching their distended bellies and burping gently. You can always whip up a quick snack later if the situation calls for it.

(Extract from *How to be a Man* by John Birmingham and Dick Flinthart)

HOW TO BE HER KITCHEN LOVE GOD

Kitchen hygiene

Basic hygiene rules are important – after all, you don't want to be known as the so-called friend who gave all his mates food poisoning. Plus it isn't going to impress her much when, instead of her arms around you,

DON'T FORGET THAT YOU HAVE TO <u>SERVE</u> THE FOOD AS WELL

You can get away with Salvation Army stuff when you're a poor and shaggy student, but if you've got an actual job and an income, it looks much more convincing if your plates match, if your glasses are all from the same set, and all of your cutlery has the same pattern. Don't overdo it, though. You are, after all, a man. It's the practicality of the situation men are supposed to master. If you actually own your own full Wedgwood dinner set and matched crystal glasses, don't get it out for a casual dinner. You're only going to frighten your guest or make her think you are a bit of a closet case. Simple matched ceramic plates and half-way decent glasses or goblets will do very nicely.

(Extract from *How to be a Man* by John Birmingham and Dick Flinthart)

Keeping your kitchen clean will cut down on incidents of food poisoning and will usually stop maggots from popping up to cha-cha-cha in the corners. Maggots are very off-putting even to the most determinedly romantic.

(Extract from *How to be a Man* by John Birmingham and Dick Flinthart)

she spends the night with them clutched around the toilet bowl.

Always wash your hands before handling food and between handling different types of food, such as raw and cooked meat. Keep cuts and grazes covered with a waterproof plaster.

Girls are impressed by the strangest things. Here are the rules for mastering germs in the kitchen.

● ● ●

Except where otherwise noted all your dishes and pans should be washed in detergent and very hot water. They should then be rinsed in really hot water, and left to drain on a dish-rack. Wipe all your counters and surfaces with disinfectant after each use. Dismantle the stove-top and clean it completely at least once every six months. Empty the fridge, clean it thoroughly, and wipe the interior with vanilla essence (mostly alcohol – strong disinfectant that smells really groovy) at least once every three months. And for God's sake, get rid of that weird greenish-black stuff in the bottom of the salad compartment.

● ● ●

Meat and poultry should never be cut on the same board as foodstuffs that are not going to be cooked, such as salad vegetables and breads. Also, leftover cooked meats should be returned to the refrigerator reasonably promptly, in a sealed container. For later use, leftovers should be very thoroughly reheated to prevent the growth of exciting things like salmonella. And you should never, ever, under any circumstances use anything from a tin which appears to be holed, rusted or bloated.

(Extract from *How to be a Man*
by John Birmingham and
Dick Flinthart)

HOW TO BE HER KITCHEN LOVE GOD

COOL THINGS
YOU CAN DO IN YOUR KITCHEN

Cooking itself is actually a whole lot simpler than it looks to most people. The trick is to see it not as a single, mysterious process which converts mere ingredients into food, but as a set of short, simple operations which are performed in an appropriate order to achieve best effect. A short list and description of some basic cooking techniques follows. Of course, there's about a zillion different techniques and variations in each of the world's great cuisines, and there's at least 20 really different and interesting cuisine styles, you could make a career out of learning this stuff – but not out of this book!

Dicing

Use your cleaver. Hold the stuff on the cutting board with your off-hand, fingers tucked up claw-style rather than stretched out, and slide the material under the cleaver as you cut. In your dominant hand, you hold the cleaver with your index finger on the uppermost corner at the top, your palm wrapped round the spine, the handle pointing towards you. As your off-hand slides the stuff under the cleaver, you rapidly raise and lower the cleaver with a simple wrist action, pivoting it around the lower corner at the top end – like a paper guillotine, if you can imagine that. Get the hang of this technique and you'll be awed at how quickly you can vanquish a bag of carrots. Same basic technique works when you're using one of those lovely, triangular bladed chef's knives.

Stir-frying

Calls for maybe 2 tablespoons of peanut oil in the bottom of the wok. Crank up the heat until the oil smokes. Never stir-fry more than a decent handful of meat at any one time, and add the vegetables and sauces only after the meat is lightly fried; you really only want the veggies warmed through, so that they keep their crispness. Keep the whole lot in constant motion, either with your wooden spoons or more flashily by 'flipping' the wok as you would a frying pan with a pancake.

Deep frying

Not something you should be doing a lot of, as it can make for fattening, unhealthy foods. When you do it , use clean oil, and use just enough to mostly cover whatever it is you're frying. Very high heat is necessary, and the food should not be added until the oil is at the right temperature. (Test by very, very carefully allowing a single drop of water into the oil. If it hisses, spits and explodes, things are ready to go. Use your tongs, or preferably, your weird metal-mesh ladle for getting things into and out of the oil.)

Frying

Calls for a little butter in the fry-pan (screw the cholesterol; margarine tastes like shit) and medium heat. Use your spatula to prevent the food sticking to the pan, although the butter, the use of medium heat, and a well-prepared pan will go a long way to help.

HOW TO BE HER KITCHEN LOVE GOD

Steaming

Put the food into one of those bamboo steamers. Put about a centimetre of water into the bottom of the wok, and turn up the heat. When the water is boiling happily, put the steamer in, with its lid on, and cover up the wok as well. A two-person serving of vegetables will steam very nicely within 60 seconds. Dumplings will need about 3 minutes.

Poaching

Lightly simmering in liquid – usually water. Produces very nasty eggs, but you can get some interesting effects with other foods if you use wine as your liquid. Use your medium saucepan, and just enough liquid to half-cover whatever you're poaching. Don't go for a full, savage boil – try to keep the liquid gently simmering. Poaching usually doesn't take more than 3 minutes.

Baking

Application of all-round heat in the oven. Usually for cakes and breads, to drive off the moisture in the dough or batter, and to coagulate the protein in the flour to hold the whole thing in shape. Oddly, though, if you prepare whole fish in this manner with a little aluminium foil to keep the moisture in, it's referred to as 'baked fish'. If you do the same thing with any other meat or fowl, however, the process is called 'roasting'. Work that one out.

HOW TO BE HER KITCHEN LOVE GOD

Roasting (see Baking)

Takes quite a long time, and requires careful observation if your going to produce a roast which is crisply glazed outside, and moistly tender inside. Easiest way of achieving this is to slow-roast the beast in a roasting pan, whilst covered with foil, at a relatively low temperature. Then, when the juices that run out after you poke the thing with a skewer are clear and colourless, remove the foil, and crank up the heat up to bastissimo for about 5–10 minutes. This should crisp up the outside quite nicely.

Boiling

For pasta and rice especially. (Although you really should think about getting a rice cooker.) Crank up the stove, get a half-pot of water so hot that it's jumping around in the saucepan, bubbling and roiling, then throw in your food and watch it cook. Anyone who boils sausages or meat is weird.

Whisking, beating and blending

Variations on a theme. Generally, the idea is either to aerate or thoroughly mix whatever it is you're working on Should always be done with a light, rapid action from the wrist. Electric implements can be an enormous help here. Always whisk, beat or blend in a bowl at least a size larger than you would think necessary at first glance – it minimises fallout.

(Extract from *How to be a Man*
by John Birmingham and Dick Flinthart)

Basic recipes

Stocks and sauces are used to enhance a host of dishes. These can be bought ready-made from the supermarket or you can make your own. Quite often, it's rushing to prepare a sauce that spoils it. Fortunately, most of these and the stocks can be prepared in advance and reheated when needed. Here is a useful selection.

VEGETABLE STOCK

MAKES: **1.1 LITRES/2 PINTS**
PREPARATION TIME: **10 MINUTES**
COOKING TIME: **35 MINUTES**

- 225g/8oz onions, peeled
- 225g/8oz celery sticks
- 225g/8oz leeks, trimmed
- 225g/8oz carrots, peeled
- 1.75 litres/3 pints cold water
- 2 bay leaves
- a few fresh thyme sprigs
- small bunch fresh parsley
- 10 black peppercorns
- ½ tsp sea salt

1 Roughly chop the onions, celery, leeks and carrots. Put the vegetables in a large saucepan with the water, herbs, peppercorns and salt. Bring slowly to the boil and skim the surface. Partially cover the pan and simmer for 30 minutes; check the seasoning.

2 Strain the stock through a fine sieve into a bowl and allow to cool. Refrigerate for up to three days. Use as required.

HOW TO BE HER KITCHEN LOVE GOD

CHICKEN STOCK

MAKES: **1.1 LITRES/2 PINTS**
PREPARATION TIME: **10 MINUTES**
COOKING TIME: **3 HOURS, APPROX.**

- 225g/8oz onions, peeled
- 150g/5oz leeks, trimmed
- 225g/8oz celery sticks
- 1.6kg/3½lb raw chicken bones
- 3 litres/5 pints cold water
- 1 bouquet garni (2 bay leaves, few thyme sprigs, small bunch of parsley)
- 1 tsp black peppercorns
- ½ tsp sea salt

1 Roughly chop the onions, leeks and celery. Put the vegetables in a large saucepan with the chicken bones, water, bouquet garni, peppercorns and salt. Bring slowly to the boil and skim the surface. Partially cover the pan and simmer gently for about 3 hours; check the seasoning.

2 Strain the stock through a fine sieve into a bowl and cool quickly. Refrigerate for up to three days. Remove the fat from the surface and use the stock as required.

HOW TO BE HER KITCHEN LOVE GOD

FISH STOCK

MAKES: **900 ML/1½ PINTS**
PREPARATION TIME: **10 MINUTES**
COOKING TIME: **35 MINUTES**

- 900g/2lb fish bones and trimmings
- 2 carrots, peeled and chopped
- 2 celery sticks, sliced
- 900ml/1½ pints cold water
- 1 bouquet garni
- 6 white peppercorns
- ½ tsp sea salt

1 Wash and dry the fish bones and trimmings and place in a large saucepan. Add the vegetables to the pan with the water, bouquet garni, peppercorns and salt. Bring slowly to the boil; skim. Cover and gently simmer for about 30 minutes.

2 Strain the stock through a fine sieve into a bowl and check the seasoning. Cool quickly, then refrigerate for up to two days. Use as required.

HOW
TO
BE
HER
KITCHEN LOVE GOD

MEAT STOCK

MAKES: **900ML/1½ PINTS**
PREPARATION TIME: **10 MINUTES**
COOKING TIME: **4–5 HOURS**

- 450g/1lb stewing meat, cut into pieces
- 450g/1lb meat bones
- 1 large onion, peeled and sliced
- 1 large carrot, peeled and sliced
- 2 celery sticks, sliced
- 2 litres/3½ pints cold water
- 1 bouquet garni
- 1 tsp black peppercorns
- ½ tsp sea salt

1 Place the meat and bones in a roasting tin and roast at 220°C/425°F/gas mark 7 for 30–40 minutes until well browned, turning occasionally.

2 Put the meat and bones in a large saucepan with the vegetables, water, bouquet garni, peppercorns and salt. Bring slowly to the boil and skim the surface. Partially cover the pan and simmer gently for at least 4 hours; check the seasoning.

3 Strain the stock through a fine sieve into a bowl and cool quickly. Refrigerate for up to three days. Remove the fat layer from the surface and use the stock as required.

HOW TO BE HER KITCHEN LOVE GOD

GRAVY

A rich gravy is usually served with a roast. Try to make it in the roasting tin while the meat is resting.

1 Carefully pour or skim off the fat from the tin, draining it off in one corner and leaving the sediment behind. Place the tin on the hob over a medium heat and pour in 300–450ml/ $\frac{1}{2}$–$\frac{3}{4}$ pint vegetable water from drained green vegetables, or the chicken, vegetable or meat stock, as appropriate.

2 Stir thoroughly, scraping up the sediment from the base of the tin and boil steadily until the gravy is a rich brown colour. Pour into a warmed gravy boat and serve.

SIMPLE WHITE SAUCE

MAKES: **300ML/½ PINT**
PREPARATION TIME: **5 MINUTES**
COOKING TIME: **5 MINUTES**

- 15g/½ oz butter
- 15g/½ oz plain flour
- 300ml/½ pint milk
- salt and pepper
- freshly grated nutmeg

1 Melt the butter in a saucepan, stir in the flour and cook, stirring for 1 minute until cooked but not coloured. Remove from the heat and gradually pour in the milk, whisking constantly. Season lightly with salt, pepper and nutmeg.

2 Return to the heat and cook, stirring, until the sauce is thickened and smooth. Simmer gently for 2 minutes.

HOW TO BE HER KITCHEN LOVE GOD

FRESH TOMATO SAUCE

SERVES: **4**
PREPARATION TIME: **10 MINUTES**
COOKING TIME: **30 MINUTES, APPROX.**

- 900g/2lb vine-ripened tomatoes, roughly chopped
- 2 tbsp extra virgin olive oil
- 2 garlic cloves, peeled and crushed
- grated zest of 1 lemon
- 1 tsp dried oregano
- 2 tbsp fresh basil, chopped
- salt and pepper
- pinch of sugar, to taste (*optional*)

1 Place the tomatoes in a saucepan with the olive oil, garlic, lemon zest and oregano. Bring to the boil, cover and simmer gently for 20 minutes.

2 Add the chopped basil, salt and pepper to taste and a little sugar, if required. Simmer, uncovered, for a further 10 minutes or until the sauce is slightly thickened. If a smooth sauce is preferred, pass through a sieve and reheat before serving.

HOW TO BE HER KITCHEN LOVE GOD

RICH CHOCOLATE SAUCE

SERVES: **6**
PREPARATION TIME: **5 MINUTES**
COOKING TIME: **5 MINUTES**

- 125g/4oz good-quality dark chocolate with a minimum of 70% cocoa solids, in pieces
- 150ml/5fl oz water
- 25g/1oz unsalted butter
- 2 tbsp Grand Marnier or other liqueur of your choice

1 Put the chocolate in a small pan with the water. Stir constantly over a low heat until the chocolate is melted, then bring to the boil, stirring.

2 Let it bubble for 1 minute, then remove from the heat and stir in the butter and liqueur.

HOW TO BE HER KITCHEN LOVE GOD

FLAVOURED BUTTERS

**To make these, use unsalted butter at room temperature
and allow 25g/1oz per person.**

1 Beat in the flavourings by hand or in a food processor. Turn on
to cling film, shape into a log and chill in the fridge for at least
1 hour.

Add the following flavourings to 125g/4oz butter:

Herb Butter

Add 2 tbsp chopped mixed fresh herbs, such as flat-leafed
parsley, chervil and tarragon, plus a squeeze of lemon juice.

Garlic Butter

Add 1 crushed garlic clove and 2 tsp chopped fresh parsley or
chervil.

HOW TO BE HER KITCHEN LOVE GOD

Wine tips

There is an amazing selection of wines to choose from these days, whether you are buying from your local off-licence or a supermarket. Helpful point-of-sale information is usually given, including what type of food to serve the wine with.

There are no hard and fast rules but, generally, red wine tastes better with red meat, while white wine goes down well with fish, chicken and light meats. Obviously, if you know she hates white wine and you're making a fish dish, then you could try a light red wine instead.

If you want to go the whole hog and serve an aperitif, then a chilled dry sherry is perfect, as is a glass of champagne or sparkling wine. Avoid serving a sweet drink or one with a high alcohol content before eating, as they tend to take the edge off your appetite. Plus you don't want everyone to be plastered before you serve up the main course.

Port is the traditional drink to serve with cheese at the end of the meal but, if you prefer, a full-bodied red wine will taste good, too.

The most important thing to remember is to serve your wine at the right temperature. White wine and champagne should be served chilled, while red wine should be at room temperature. Leave red wine to stand in a warm room for 1–2 hours but do not have it in a hot spot, say right by a radiator. Uncork it at least 1 hour before serving.

You might think about getting a couple of champagne glasses. Champagne is what women drink instead of beer.

(Extract from *How to be a Man* by John Birmingham and Dick Flinthart)

If you are having a party or a lot of dinner guests and you have got several bottles of white wine to keep cool, then you can buy large bags of ice from off-licences, supermarkets or wine merchants. The best place to keep the wine is in a bath or large plastic container, filled with the ice and cold water. The ice and water should come up to the bottle necks. Do this at least an hour before the party starts.

A word about clearing up

As you return triumphant to the kitchen after your darling has feasted, you may be tempted to shut the door and promise you'll clear up tomorrow.

Don't. The very best idea is to tidy up as you go along. If you have a dishwasher, empty it before you start cooking, and fill it up with dirty utensils as you go along. Or flood the sink with hot water and dump your used citrus zester in it until you have a spare moment. Then wash it up. Throw your potato peelings in the bin as a matter of urgency. The excuse that you haven't time is nonsense – there is always a spare minute during the actual cooking. If you really truly are rushed off your feet until the coffee hour, then at least stack everything neatly in the sink and wipe down the surfaces.

This isn't in case your mother decides to pop around. It is in case your woman starts to fret about crumbs on the hob. Women tend to be perfectionists. They hate unfinished business. Some find it hard to get smoochy when the kitchen looks as if a bomb and a hurricane have hit it. They itch to get things straight and say things like, 'It'll only take me a minute.' You understand what I'm saying. She'll be scrubbing and polishing till 2am and

HOW TO BE HER KITCHEN LOVE GOD

by the time she's finished, you'll be sulking or asleep. Meanwhile, she'll be exhausted and/or irked that you didn't tidy up yourself. Either way, the likelihood of passion diminishes. Whereas 'tidy as you go' and both parties have a clear diary…

Strange but true …
nothing about your cooking
will impress a woman more than
your ability to leave behind a
neat and tidy kitchen.

(Extract from *How to be a Man*
by John Birmingham and
Dick Flinthart)

HOW
TO
BE
HER
KITCHEN LOVE GOD

- Vodka-spiked Cherry Tomatoes
- Gravlax with Mustard Sauce and Brown Bread
- Asparagus with Toasted Almonds
- Spicy Prunes Wrapped in Bacon
- Warm Oysters with Shallot Vinegar
- Basic Rare Steak
- Figs and Parma Ham with Dolcelatte
- Honey-glazed Orange and Rosemary Chicken
- Sinful Monkfish
- Venison Steaks with a Rich Red Wine Sauce
- Satan's Own Chocolate Mousse
- Hot Sticky Bananas with Ice Cream
- Dark Chocolate Pots with Sticky Dates
- Tiramisu Snaps
- Cocktail Sorbet

2. COOKING
to seduce

A man cooking appeals to the Neanderthal in every woman. Women adore the idea that you have gone hunting, bopped a woolly mammoth on the head, hauled it back to your cave, and are now skinning it over the fire, all in the name of love or lust, whilst she lolls around eating berries. Admittedly, you have more likely driven to Waitrose, plucked a few chicken breasts out of the refrigerated cabinet, plonked the bags in the boot, tootled home and hauled your frying pan out of the cupboard, but the principle is the same. You are thinking of how to please her. You are showing your devotion by providing for her. Women may be independent and ambitious but they aren't masochists – no one-wants to do everything for themselves.

When you cook for a woman she sees a lot more than food on the table. It suggests you're a great guy. Why? Because, unlike the majority of men, you aren't sitting in the pub with the rugby crew downing your eleventh pint; you're hunched over a chopping board

Remember all those films where food and sex are brought into combination? All the sequences you've seen with whipped cream and cherries, noodles and canoodling? It's an established idea within our culture – the sexuality of food. Men who know how to stimulate the senses with food – smell, taste, sight and touch. Men who are prepared to indulge in the sensuality of a fine meal are (in the mind of women) men who may well be able to demonstrate sensitivity, creativity and sensuality in other, more intimate situations. 'Men who can cook,' said a girlfriend when we asked her 'Well, you know – they're just...' And then she produced a slow smile that could have ignited the Pope's boxers.

(Extract from *How to be a Man* by John Birmingham and Dick Flinthart)

snipping parsley and squinting at a recipe book. To women, that's endearing. It is also infinitely more appealing than being pompously wined and tediously dined in a stuffy restaurant. Any old berk with a fat wallet can book a table and order the Chateauneuf du Pape. But only a special kind of man dons an apron and sweats with the shallots.

When a man cooks dinner, women suspect you of all sorts of hidden talents. To be blunt, they see your cooking skills as an indication of your horizontal prowess.

Quite apart from the heart-warming boost you'll achieve by impressing a babe with the quality of your cooking, this sort of in-house entertaining has some built in tactical advantages in the love stakes. There will be wine, naturally. Lots of it. She's relaxed. You're relaxed. There's no question about who's paying for what. Your entire bar stock (carefully supplemented for the evening) is close at hand. Atmosphere is easy to achieve with a few candles and some thoughtfully chosen music. Most importantly, there will be **absolutely no embarrassment** about trying to get her back to your place for the night. **She's already there!**

(Extract from *How to be a Man* by John Birmingham and Dick Flinthart)

A really good meal is practically a metaphor for sex in its own right. From the foreplay of soups and entrées, which build the appetite and arouse the senses, to the climactic satisfaction of the main course, down through the lazy, sensual after-play of dessert. A well constructed dinner is a complete seduction, engaging the senses to their fullest and delivering a rich palette of pleasures to the participants. It **will** get you laid.

(Extract from *How to be a Man* by John Birmingham and Dick Flinthart)

KNOW YOUR TARGET

No point serving mushrooms if she hates the things, right? Worse still, if she's seriously allergic to something you're cooking, you'll discover there's nothing like a trip to A & E to ruin the mood.

(Extract from *How to be a Man* by John Birmingham and Dick Flinthart)

That dash of coriander suggests a delicate touch, the haphazard way you throw in the mushrooms shows heartiness of appetite, that sizzle of olive oil reveals a sense of humour, confidence, sensuality, a willingness to get down and dirty… You see how easy it is to get carried away.

All recipes serve 2.

SNACKS

Never neglect this one. Best if you've got a few put aside in advance, just in case. Snacks are for those moments late at night, when you need just a little extra on your side to convince her to stay for another bottle of wine, or a video, or whatever. They're also for those times when you need a little renewal of energy – say about two hours after you finally hit the bed.

● ● ●

Just about any sort of finger food will do, of course – tasty cheeses, fresh bread, antipasto and fruit – but it's always impressive if you can whip together a couple of personalised treats.

(Extract from *How to be a Man* by John Birmingham and Dick Flinthart)

HOW TO BE HER KITCHEN LOVE GOD

VODKA-SPIKED CHERRY TOMATOES

Vodka shoots down the throat as you bite into these juicy little tomatoes, leaving you both with a warm glow.

PREPARATION TIME: **10 MINUTES**

- 12 cherry tomatoes
- vodka, chilled

1 Cut a cross in the top of each tomato, squeeze it open and carefully drizzle a little vodka into each one. The alcohol will sink into the middle of the tomato. Chill until needed, then serve in a shallow bowl.

GRAVLAX WITH MUSTARD SAUCE AND BROWN BREAD

This delicious starter of luscious gravlax, drizzled with a tangy sauce, will have her begging for the next course, and maybe even you.

PREPARATION TIME: **10 MINUTES**

- 2 tbsp Dijon mustard
- 2 tsp red wine vinegar
- 2 tsp soft brown sugar
- 5 tbsp olive oil
- handful fresh dill, chopped
- sea salt flakes and freshly ground black pepper, to season
- 4 slices gravlax
- brown bread-and-butter triangles, to serve

1 Put the mustard, red wine vinegar and sugar into a bowl and mix together. Slowly add the oil, whisking continuously. Add the dill and season. Serve with the gravlax and brown bread and butter.

ASPARAGUS WITH TOASTED ALMONDS

Eating with your fingers is the key to seductive dining, and with this you can feed each other spear by spear. Just don't get carried away and poke her in the eye!

PREPARATION TIME: **10 MINUTES**
COOKING TIME: **10 MINUTES**

- 225g/8oz asparagus
- 75g/3oz whole almonds, roughly chopped
- 50g/2oz butter
- sea salt, freshly ground black pepper, to season

1 Bring a pan of water to the boil and cook the asparagus until tender, but still firm (about 10 minutes).

2 Place the almonds into a dry frying pan and toast them over a medium heat for a minute until golden brown.

3 Pile the asparagus onto a plate and top with the almonds. Add the butter to the pan and melt until bubbling, then drizzle over the asparagus. Season.

HOW TO BE HER KITCHEN LOVE GOD

SPICY PRUNES WRAPPED IN BACON

Bite into crispy bacon on the outside to reveal a juicy, succulent prune on the inside – together these make a tempting combination.

PREPARATION TIME: **5 MINUTES**
COOKING TIME: **1 HOUR**

- 10 streaky bacon rashers
- 10 Californian prunes, stoned
- Worcester sauce

1 Preheat the oven to 200°C/400°F/gas mark 6.

2 Wrap a rasher of bacon around each prune and impale on cocktail sticks. Bake for 1 hour until the bacon is crisp. Serve on a platter with a bowl of Worcester sauce and drizzle with more sauce.

HOW TO BE HER KITCHEN LOVE GOD

WARM OYSTERS WITH SHALLOT VINEGAR

Oysters are often thought to be aphrodisiacs, and you should find your desire levels rising as you pop them in your mouth and let them sliver down.

PREPARATION TIME: **15 MINUTES**
COOKING TIME: **4–5 MINUTES**

- 4 tbsp red wine vinegar
- 1 large or 2 small shallots, finely chopped
- freshly ground black pepper, to season
- 12 oysters
- coarse salt to serve (*optional*)

1 Mix the vinegar and shallots in a non-metallic bowl. Season with black pepper and, if you have time, leave to stand at room temperature for a while so that the flavours can combine.

2 Rinse the oysters under cold water and spread a layer of salt (if using) over two large plates.

3 Preheat a large frying pan and place the oysters in it with a splash of water. Cover and cook just long enough for the shells to open and for the oysters to slightly warm (4–5 minutes).

4 Using a sharp knife, remove the top shells and place the bottom, flesh-filled shells on the plates. Serve immediately with the shallot vinegar.

BASIC RARE STEAK

This is a much under-rated dish. It is also not easy to do well. Good steak should always be served rare – dark, perhaps even charred outside, and pink and juicy inside. Pick a good cut – rump as a minimum, fillet better, rib eye better still – and make sure it's at least 3cm thick at the absolute minimum. Don't mess around with the supermarket when you're trying to impress someone; go and have a talk with your local butcher.

With the general downturn in consumption of red meat, a really good steak is getting harder to find in restaurants around the country. And to be fair, you don't need to eat them all that often. However, they are an excellent source of iron and protein, and for obvious reasons, many, many women occasionally find themselves craving a good piece of meat. Learn to do this one right.

• ⊗ •

1 Put two cloves of crushed garlic in a small jar with some light vegetable oil, at least 24 hours before you want to cook your steak. (Not olive oil. Good olive oil is a dressing oil. It's cold-pressed and starts to burn at too low a temperature.) Prior to cooking the steak, you should also rub it down with a clove of crushed garlic.

2 Crank up your cast-iron frying pan to Supernova, with just a couple of teaspoons of oil across the bottom to stop things sticking. Grab your steak, and slap it down in the middle of the pan. (Lots of hissing, smoke and steam.) At this time, add about a level dessert-spoon of coarse-ground, fresh black pepper.

3 If your pan is correctly heated, and your steak is between 3cm and 4cm thick, you should need to leave it for at most 2 minutes. Then quickly turn it over, and sear the other side in the same manner, cooking it just a little longer as the pan will have lost some of this heat. Don't turn it again. Whip the pan off the heat, and put the steak on the plate. Using the pan juices add just a little butter and garlic, and quickly fry up a handful of fresh, sliced mushrooms to accompany the steak. Serve with a baked potato and a large, fresh green salad. A nice, big Cabernet Sauvignon makes an excellent accompaniment.

4 If everything has gone well, the steak will be absolutely fantastic – meltingly tender inside, savoury, slightly crisp and smoky on the outside. You probably won't manage this the first two or three times you try it, so practise this recipe for yourself before trying it on anyone else. And never, ever, grill a really good quality steak – grilling dries it out and the steak behaves like leather.

(Extract from *How to be a Man*
by John Birmingham and Dick Flinthart)

FIGS AND PARMA HAM WITH DOLCELATTE

Have a feel of your figs first – you'll know that they are sweet and succulent if they are soft and squashy to the touch.

PREPARATION TIME: **10 MINUTES**

- 175g/6oz dolcelatte or other creamy blue cheese
- 2 tbsp lemon juice
- salt and freshly ground black pepper, to season
- 6 paper-thin slices Parma ham
- 6 ripe figs
- parsley or mint sprigs, to garnish

1 Put the cheese in a bowl with the lemon juice. Using a fork, lightly mash to give a coarse paste (add a little cold water, if necessary, to give a spreading consistency). Season with salt and freshly ground black pepper and transfer the mixture to a small bowl.

2 Arrange the Parma ham slices on a serving platter or individual plates. Halve or quarter the figs lengthwise and arrange with the ham. Serve with the dolcelatte mixture, garnished with parsley or mint sprigs.

3 Alternatively, prepare the figs by making three cuts into the flesh of each, almost to the base, to make wedges. Open these out like petals. Arrange the opened figs with the ham, and spoon a little cheese mixture into the centre of each.

HONEY-GLAZED ORANGE AND ROSEMARY CHICKEN

Before you attempt to have your fill of her, let her have her fill of this saucy chicken dish with its citrus-sweet flavour.

PREPARATION TIME: **15 MINUTES (PLUS 30 MINUTES MARINATING)**
COOKING TIME: **35–45 MINUTES**

- 1 orange
- 3 tbsp runny honey
- 2 sprigs fresh rosemary
- 4 chicken pieces (legs, thighs or breasts)
- 3 garlic cloves, peeled and left whole
- freshly ground black pepper, to season
- 500g/1lb new potatoes
- sea salt flakes

1 Preheat the oven to 200°C/400°F/gas mark 6. Cut 2 strips of zest from the orange, using a vegetable peeler, then chop this into thin strips. Squeeze the juice from one half of the orange into a bowl. Add the zest, honey and rosemary, and mix.

2 Cut the other orange half into thin slices, add to the bowl along with the chicken pieces and the garlic, season well. Toss to coat then cover and leave to marinate for a least 30 minutes in the fridge. Transfer the chicken and marinade to a roasting dish and cook for 35–45 minutes, basting occasionally.

3 Meanwhile, boil the new potatoes for 15 minutes, until tender. Drain and put in an ovenproof dish. Drizzle with a little olive oil and toss in sea salt flakes. Serve with the chicken and a mixed green salad.

SINFUL MONKFISH

Mix pleasure with pain when you bite into this devilish dish. As the chillies are grilled and skinned, they lose a little of their ferocity, but none of their flavour.

PREPARATION TIME: **20 MINUTES**
COOKING TIME: **15 MINUTES**

- 225g/8oz monkfish or other firm white fish, filleted
- 2–4 large red chillies
- 15g/½ oz butter
- 2 tbsp extra virgin olive oil
- 1 small onion, chopped
- 1 garlic clove, thinly sliced
- 1 tbsp capers, rinsed and drained
- zest of ½ a small lemon, grated
- 175g/6oz dried pasta
- 2 tbsp fresh mixed herbs, such as parsley, coriander and mint, chopped
- ½ tsp lemon juice
- salt and freshly ground black pepper, to season

1 Preheat the grill to hot. Cut the monkfish into thin slices and set aside. Grill the chillies whole, turning occasionally, until their skins are blackened and blistered. This will take about 10 minutes. Carefully remove and discard the skins, then slit each chilli open lengthways and rinse out the seeds under the cold tap. Dry on kitchen paper and cut the flesh into thin strips lengthways. Bring a large saucepan of water to the boil for the pasta.

2 Heat the butter and oil in a frying pan. Add the onion and cook on a medium heat for 5 minutes, stirring frequently, until soft. Stir in the garlic and cook for a further minute. Increase the heat to medium-high and add the fish to the pan. Cook, stirring, for 3–4 minutes until firm and opaque, then lower the heat and stir in the capers, chillies and lemon zest. Remove from the heat.

3 Just before serving, cook the pasta according to the packet instructions. Drain thoroughly and transfer to a large bowl.

4 To serve, return the fish to the heat. Gently heat through and, when hot, remove from the heat and stir in the herbs and lemon juice. Season, then add to the pasta and toss lightly to mix. Serve immediately.

DO WE HAVE TO TELL YOU TO MIND THE SPICES?

You may be an iron-gulleted chilli monster but she's probably not. Also, the effects of overly spicy food on your digestive tract, especially if combined with vigorous exercise, can make the bed a pretty nasty place to be a couple of hours later.

(Extract from *How to be a Man* by John Birmingham and Dick Flinthart)

HOW TO BE HER KITCHEN LOVE GOD

VENISON STEAKS WITH A RICH RED WINE SAUCE

This unusual, meaty dish is rich in iron, which will help you keep your strength up – and you're going to need it later.

PREPARATION TIME: **10 MINUTES**
COOKING TIME: **10 MINUTES, APPROX.**

- 75g/3oz butter
- 2 venison steaks

For the sauce
- 150ml/5fl oz red wine
- 1 red onion, peeled and sliced
- 2 anchovy fillets, finely chopped
- bunch fresh flat-leaf parsley, chopped
- sea salt
- freshly ground black pepper
- lemon juice, to taste

1 Melt the butter in a large, heavy-based frying pan. Add the venison steaks and sauté for 5 minutes on each side. Then leave them on a plate to rest.

2 Add the red wine to the pan and stir to dislodge any crispy bits, cooking for a few minutes to reduce the alcohol. Add the onion and cook briefly. Add the anchovy, parsley and seasoning. Pour in the lemon juice, then serve the sauce with the venison.

SATAN'S OWN CHOCOLATE MOUSSE

Chances are, she'll hate you for this. But it will be a pleasant, obsessive sort of hatred not unmingled with lust, because this mousse is completely undeniable. Refusing to eat it is unthinkable, despite the fact that it contains more kilo-joules and cholesterol than the collective arse-end of an entire Oprah audience.

• ⚔ •

- 1 tbsp brandy per person
- 6 coffee beans
- one egg per person
- 240ml/8fl oz double cream per person, plus extra 240ml/8fl oz for every two people
- caster sugar
- vanilla essence
- 150g/5oz dark chocolate per person

1 Prepare the brandy 24 hours in advance by soaking six good quality coffee beans in it

2 Break the eggs, separating the whites from the yolks. Put the yolks away, add one dessertspoon of sugar for each egg to the egg whites, and whisk them until they stand up in stiff, frothy peaks. Put the whipped egg whites in the fridge.

☞

3 Now whip 240ml/8fl oz of cream per person, with just a teaspoon of vanilla essence and a dessertspoon of sugar for every 580ml/16fl oz of cream. Whip it until, like the egg whites, it forms stiff peaks. Gently, carefully, thoroughly fold the cream into the bowl containing the egg whites, and refrigerate the lot.

4 Break up all the chocolate. Put the remaining cream in a medium saucepan with the brandy (remove the coffee beans first) over a low heat. Stir in the chocolate and the egg yolks until you have a thick, smooth, dark sauce. Turn off the heat, and let the sauce come to just above room temperature.

5 Now gently fold the sauce through the egg whites and cream until the mixture is evenly coloured. Spoon into individual serving dishes, and refrigerate. Serve with a dollop of whipped cream, some grated dark chocolate, and a couple of Italian sponge-finger biscuits.

(Extract from *How to be a Man*
by John Birmingham and Dick Flinthart)

HOT STICKY BANANAS WITH ICE CREAM

A sexy supper has just got to have a banana in there somewhere, and if you still think your energy levels need a boost, then these sticky, sweet servings will help.

PREPARATION TIME: **5 MINUTES**
COOKING TIME: **5 MINUTES**

- 2 firm, but ripe, bananas
- 50g/2oz unsalted butter
- 2 tbsp dark brown sugar
- 2 tbsp orange marmalade
- good quality vanilla ice cream

1 Peel and cut the bananas diagonally into four. Heat the butter in a frying pan, add bananas, sugar and marmalade and cook for about 5 minutes, turning frequently, until bananas are golden brown and sticky. Serve on balls of ice cream, drizzling juices from the pan over the top.

2 For a frisky accompaniment, throw 3 tablespoons of citrus vodka, 125ml/4fl oz cranberry juice and 75ml/3fl oz orange juice into a cocktail shaker. Shake and pour into tall glasses, adding a lime wedge.

HOW TO BE HER KITCHEN LOVE GOD

DARK CHOCOLATE POTS WITH STICKY DATES

One shot glass of this deliciously rich dessert is enough, but you may want to make more so you can come back for afters.

MAKES: **2–4 SHOT GLASSES**
PREPARATION TIME: **15–20 MINUTES**
COOKING TIME: **10 MINUTES**

50g/2oz dates (medjool are best)
15g/½ oz butter
50ml/2fl oz double cream
50ml/2fl oz crème fraîche
125g/4oz dark chocolate
1 small-sized egg
pinch of salt
1 drop vanilla extract
chocolate shavings, to decorate

1   Stone and roughly chop the dates. Melt the butter in a pan, add the dates and sauté for a few minutes. Transfer to a plate.

2   Put the cream and crème fraîche into the same pan, heat gently. Break the chocolate into small pieces and add to the warm cream. Stir over a gentle heat for a few minutes. Take off the heat and continue to stir until all the chocolate has melted.

3   Lightly beat the egg, add to the chocolate with the salt and vanilla and return to a gentle heat; stir until smooth (about 2 minutes).

4   Divide the sautéed dates between the glasses and cover with the chocolate mixture. Decorate with white and dark chocolate shavings.

HOW TO BE HER KITCHEN LOVE GOD

TIRAMISU SNAPS

Even more chocolate and more stickiness! The coffee-flavoured cream tastes wonderful with the crunchy brandy snaps.

PREPARATION TIME: **15 MINUTES**

- 2 tbsp strong coffee
- 150ml/5fl oz whipping cream
- 100g/3½ oz dark bar chocolate, broken into pieces
- 150ml/5fl oz mascarpone cheese
- 4 brandy snaps

1 Make the strong coffee and set aside to cool. Meanwhile, whip up the cream. Melt the chocolate pieces in a heatproof bowl over a saucepan of gently simmering water. Add the mascarpone cheese and the cooled coffee to the cream and mix everything together.

2 Spoon or pipe the cream into the brandy snaps. Pile up on a plate and drizzle the hot, melted chocolate over the top. Serve immediately.

COCKTAIL SORBET

Freshen up with this zingy number before you move into the bedroom. Instead of the grenadine or crème de cassis, you can use raspberry jam, strained and thinned with a little water, if you prefer.

PREPARATION TIME: **5 MINUTES**

- 500ml/17½ oz tub of orange or lemon sorbet
- 1 tbsp grenadine or crème de cassis
- 50ml/2fl oz each of vodka, tequila, champagne or sparkling wine
- 2 sprigs of fresh mint, to decorate

ABOVE ALL, HAVE FUN!

If it all looks too serious, she's going to suspect that it was hard work, which will shatter the impression of careless competence you were trying to establish. At least try to look like you enjoy what you're doing.

(Extract from *How to be a Man* by John Birmingham and Dick Flinthart)

1 Let the sorbet soften at room temperature for 10–15 minutes. Take two tall-stemmed bowls and put a couple of scoops in each, then place in the freezer. Before serving, remove the sorbets from the freezer and pour over the grenadine or crème de cassis and the other alcohol. Decorate with mint and serve.

- Banana, Mango and Pineapple Smoothie
- Bloody Mary
- Breakfast Pancakes
- Flipping Good Fillings:
  Fresh Fruit, Yogurt and Honey
  Pancakes with Mushrooms
- Scrambled Eggs with Smoked Salmon
- Sausage Patties
- Kedgeree
- Cheat's Blinis
- Filled Bagels
- Filled Croissants
- Herby Cheese on Toast
- American Style Muffins
- Chocolate Pecan Brownies

3. THE MORNING after

So, you thought the hard work was over. Not so fast. If you want to show her you're a man who can go the distance, then learn how to make a decent breakfast or brunch.

Happily, this involves less work than a full-blown dinner and is easily as impressive because it is unexpected. It proves to her that you didn't just want to get her into bed. Think of it as aftercare. It will astound and delight her, especially if you bring her the papers as well, or a flower you've picked from the garden (it's okay, we won't tell your friends).

BREAKFASTS

The importance of breakfast cannot be overstressed. If you've made the grade the night before, and that stunning babe is currently reposing in fetching disarray upon your sheets, there is nothing at all in the world more likely to score you a replay than fronting up with a platter of something tasty while she's still rubbing the sleep out of her eyes. Friends, if you meet a woman anywhere in the world who doesn't have a deep-seated weakness for a really fine breakfast brought to her in bed, take care: she is almost certainly an alien body snatcher.

(Extract from *How to be a Man* by John Birmingham and Dick Flinthart)

This advice also applies to men in a long-term relationship as well as to those cooking in hope. There's no point getting together if all romance ceases the minute she becomes a sure thing. And all romance *will* cease if you don't do loving things for her – like making her brunch.

Be assured, the health of your love life directly relates to you doing your fair share of housekeeping. She won't feel passionate towards you if she does all the chores. However, she won't regard it as your duty to make her an exotic breakfast or a fancy brunch – a man who cooks in the morning is a deliciously unexpected bonus – so imagine the gold stars you'll rack up when you do. Without meaning to sound sneaky, if you spend an hour on Sunday morning preparing a culinary feast, there is very little doubt that you will escape more humdrum tasks such as cleaning the bath. And, of course, you can serve up your creation to your darling in bed. Yourself as dessert is optional.

All the following recipes serve 2.

BANANA, MANGO AND PINEAPPLE SMOOTHIE

You'll need a blender to whizz up this refreshing, fruity drink that takes just minutes to prepare.

PREPARATION TIME: **5 MINUTES**

- 1 large banana
- 1 ripe mango
- 350ml/12fl oz chilled pineapple juice

1 Whizz together the flesh of the banana and mango and the pineapple juice in a blender until smooth. Serve over ice.

HOW TO BE HER KITCHEN LOVE GOD

BLOODY MARY

Deliciously decadent, a Bloody Mary will give you a real kick-start, especially if you have overdone it the night before.

PREPARATION TIME: **5 MINUTES**

- 2 measures of vodka
- 6 measures of tomato juice
- dash of lemon juice
- 4 dashes of Worcester sauce
- Tabasco sauce, salt and freshly ground black pepper, to taste
- lemon slices and stick of celery, to garnish

1 Shake the vodka, tomato juice, lemon juice and Worcester sauce together, seasoning to taste with the Tabasco sauce, salt and black pepper. Serve with ice, garnished with the lemon slices and celery.

HOW TO BE HER KITCHEN LOVE GOD

BREAKFAST PANCAKES

Not only are these light and fluffy, but they are also crumb-free, which makes them ideal for eating between the sheets.

PREPARATION TIME: **10 MINUTES (PLUS 30 MINUTES RESTING)**
COOKING TIME: **5 MINUTES, APPROX.**

75g/3oz self-raising flour
½ tsp bicarbonate of soda
pinch of salt
2 tbsp caster sugar (*optional*)
1 egg, beaten
150ml/5fl oz natural yogurt
150ml/5fl oz milk
a little oil (or oil and butter) for frying

1   Sift the flour, bicarbonate of soda and salt into a bowl. Stir in the sugar, if using. Make a well in the centre and add the beaten egg. Using a whisk or wooden spoon, gradually beat in the yogurt and milk to make a smooth batter. Leave to rest for 30 minutes.

2   Heat a lightly-greased, heavy-based frying pan on a fairly high heat. Pour a little of the mixture into the pan to form a small circle, or pour into heart-shaped cutters. Cook until browned underneath, with small bubbles appearing on the surface. Flip the pancake over and cook the other side. Pile the pancakes on kitchen paper as you cook the rest. Continue until all the mixture is used and serve at once.

FLIPPING GOOD FILLINGS

Fresh fruit, yogurt and honey

Decorate pancakes with fresh seasonal fruits. Add a dollop of
thick, creamy yogurt and drizzle with honey.

Pancakes with mushrooms

Omit the sugar from the pancake batter. Make the filling by
slicing some large mushrooms and frying them in butter, then
stir in chopped parsley and a little thick cream. Season with salt
and freshly ground black pepper. Serve with a dollop of cream.

SCRAMBLED EGGS WITH SMOKED SALMON

If you prefer to serve the scrambled eggs without smoked salmon, then you can jazz up this dish by adding chopped herbs to the eggs.

PREPARATION TIME: **10 MINUTES**
COOKING TIME: **3–4 MINUTES, APPROX**.

- 50g/2oz smoked salmon
- 4 eggs
- salt and freshly ground black pepper
- 25g/1oz butter
- hot buttered toast
- 2 tsp snipped chives, to garnish

1   Use scissors to snip the smoked salmon into thin strips. Set aside. Lightly beat the eggs and season with black pepper and a little salt (bear in mind that smoked salmon is quite salty).

2   Melt half the butter in a saucepan. Add the eggs and cook, stirring over a low heat until they are softly set. Remove from the heat and stir in the rest of the butter to stop the cooking process. Mix in most of the smoked salmon.

3   Serve, piled on top of hot buttered toast with the remaining salmon and chives sprinkled over as a garnish.

SAUSAGE PATTIES

These lean, herby patties make a nice change from regular sausages, and they taste particularly good with scrambled eggs.

MAKES ABOUT **9** PATTIES
PREPARATION TIME: **10 MINUTES**
COOKING TIME: **4–6 MINUTES**

2 spring onions, chopped
3–4 large sage leaves, roughly chopped
450g/1lb lean pork, roughly cubed
¼ tsp cayenne pepper
¼ tsp black pepper
sunflower oil for frying

1   Place the spring onions and sage leaves in a food processor and chop finely. Add the lean pork, cayenne pepper, black pepper and salt and blend together until well mixed and almost paste-like. Heat the oil in a heavy-based frying pan until hot. Flatten walnut-sized pieces of meat into patties and pan-fry for 2–3 minutes on each side, depending on the thickness.

HOW
TO
BE
HER
KITCHEN LOVE GOD

KEDGEREE

Indian spices add to this traditional breakfast. The ingredients include rice, eggs and fish so it is guaranteed to fill you up.

PREPARATION TIME: **10 MINUTES**
COOKING TIME: **10–15 MINUTES**

- 125g/4oz basmati rice
- 300ml/½ pint salted water
- 15g/½ oz butter
- 1 small onion, chopped
- ¼ tsp turmeric
- ½ tsp ground coriander
- ½ tsp ground cumin
- 150ml/5fl oz single cream
- 225g/8oz undyed smoked haddock, skinned
- 2 soft-boiled eggs, roughly chopped
- handful of fresh coriander leaves, roughly chopped
- freshly ground black pepper

1 Soak the basmati rice and rinse it well, then cook gently in the salted water in a covered pan for about 5–10 minutes, until all the water is absorbed. Set aside and keep hot.

2 Melt the butter in a large shallow pan and add the onion and ground spices. Sauté gently until the onion is soft, then add the cream and the fish. Poach gently for 5 minutes, then roughly flake the fish. Combine the rice and the fish and cream mixture with the eggs and most of the fresh coriander. Season to taste with freshly ground black pepper.

3 Serve hot, garnished with the remaining fresh coriander.

CHEAT'S BLINIS

Real blinis are made from yeast batter that needs to be proved then cooked on a skillet. Here is a quicker version, using shop-bought pancakes.

PREPARATION TIME: **5 MINUTES**

- 4 Scotch pancakes
- 75g/3oz smoked salmon
- 75ml/3fl oz crème fraîche
- red and black lumpfish roe or salmon eggs
- snipped chives

1 Lightly toast the pancakes and arrange the smoked salmon, crème fraîche, lumpfish roe and chives over the top.

HOW TO BE HER KITCHEN LOVE GOD

FILLED BAGELS

A Stateside favourite, bagels are something you can really get your teeth into, and you can fill them with savoury or sweet ingredients.

PREPARATION TIME: **12 MINUTES**

- 4 eggs
- 4 bagels
- 6 tbsp mayonnaise
- 2 large tomatoes, sliced
- 50g/2oz thinly sliced salami
- a few black olives, pitted and halved
- salt and freshly ground black pepper
- a handful of rocket or other salad leaves, to garnish

1 Add the eggs to a pan of boiling water and cook them for 5–6 minutes. Cool under cold running water, then shell and chop. Meanwhile, split open the bagels and either warm in the oven or lightly toast. Spread them with mayonnaise and fill with the tomatoes and salami. Top with the chopped eggs and olives, and season to taste. Garnish with rocket.

FILLED CROISSANTS

**If you want to go Continental, then choose croissants.
Using ready-made croissant dough, this stylish breakfast
is easy to prepare.**

PREPARATION TIME: **5 MINUTES**
COOKING TIME: **20 MINUTES**

- 240g pack of Kool 6 French
  Croissants dough
- 4 dried figs
- 5 slices Spanish Serrano ham,
  or Parma ham

1 Preheat the oven to 200°C/400°F/gas mark 6. Open the
  croissant dough and separate the dough triangles along the
  perforations, using a sharp knife.

2 Roughly chop the figs and tear the ham, then scatter evenly
  over the croissant dough. Loosely roll the dough from the
  broad end of the triangle (making sure the filling stays inside)
  to form a croissant shape.

3 Transfer to a baking sheet and bake in the preheated oven for
  about 20 minutes or until golden and cooked through. Serve
  immediately.

HOW TO BE HER KITCHEN LOVE GOD

HERBY CHEESE ON TOAST

Butter her up with a creamy selection of cheeses – she'll soon discover that there's more to this than your regular cheese on toast.

PREPARATION TIME: **10 MINUTES**

- 4 thick slices crusty white bread
- 150g/5oz Leerdammer cheese
- 30g/1½ oz Roquefort cheese
- 1 small fresh goats' cheese
- 15g/½ softened butter
- ½ tbsp fresh mixed herbs, chopped
- ¼ tbsp Worcester sauce
- ½ tbsp sherry
- 1 tbsp grappa
- black grapes, halved to garnish

1 Lightly toast the slices of bread. Grate the Leerdammer, put in a dish and add the Roquefort, the goats' cheese and the softened butter. Mash with a fork and mix well until you get an even cream. Add the chopped herbs and the Worcester sauce. Season with the sherry and grappa and continue to mix. Put in the fridge.

2 To serve, spread the cream mixture on the bread slices and garnish with the halved grapes.

HOW TO BE HER KITCHEN LOVE GOD

AMERICAN-STYLE MUFFINS

If you crave sweet rather than savoury, then you'll enjoy these. Add chocolate chips or blueberries to the basic mix, if you like.

MAKES **12**
PREPARATION TIME: **12 MINUTES**
COOKING TIME: **15–20 MINUTES**

- 300g/11oz plain flour
- 75g/3oz caster sugar
- 1 tbsp baking powder
- ½ tsp baking soda
- pinch of salt
- 2 eggs, beaten
- 225ml/8fl oz milk
- 1 tsp grated orange zest
- 4 tbsp melted butter
- 6 tbsp blackberry jam or marmalade

1 Preheat the oven to 200°C/400°F/gas mark 6. Mix the flour, sugar, baking powder, soda and salt together. In another bowl, beat the eggs with the milk, orange zest and melted butter.

2 Stir the egg mixture into the dried ingredients but leave it lumpy. Spoon 2 tablespoons of batter into paper cases or well-buttered deep bun tins. Add a teaspoon or two of your favourite jam or marmalade then divide the remainder of the batter between the tins. Fill to about three-quarters full. Bake them in the oven for 15–20 minutes or until a skewer inserted in the centre comes out free of batter. Cool in the tins and serve warm.

HOW
TO
BE
HER
KITCHEN LOVE GOD

CHOCOLATE PECAN BROWNIES

These taste great with a cup of coffee and, for an added treat, serve with cream, ice cream or chocolate sauce, decorated with mint.

MAKES: **6–9 BROWNIES**
PREPARATION TIME: **10 MINUTES**
COOKING TIME: **35–40 MINUTES**

- 325g/11oz plain dark chocolate, broken into pieces
- 125g/4oz butter
- 4 eggs, beaten
- 2 tsp natural vanilla essence
- 50g/2oz muscovado sugar
- ½ tsp baking powder
- 125g/4oz pecan nuts, roughly chopped
- icing sugar, to dust

1 Preheat the oven to 180°C/350°F/gas mark 4. Line a greased 9 inch square cake tin with baking parchment. Put the chocolate and butter in a saucepan and heat gently to melt. Leave to cool.

2 Put the eggs, vanilla and sugar in a large bowl and use an electric beater to whisk until pale and thick. Then whisk in the melted chocolate and butter mixture and fold in the baking powder and pecans. Pour into the prepared tin and bake for 35 to 40 minutes, until just firm. Leave to cool in the tin and then turn out and cut into squares. Dust with icing sugar.

- Vegetable and Cheese Frittata
- Thai Green Chicken Curry
- Fragrant Rice
- Hot Chilli Special
- Field Mushrooms with Oregano and Parmesan Shavings
- Scallops with Oranges and Pancetta
- Warm Chicken Waldorf Salad
- Sole with a Tomato Salsa
- Pappardelle with Bacon and Vegetables
- Lamb Cutlets with Thyme, Tomatoes and Fennel
- Chicken with Mushrooms and Tomatoes
- Mango Coulis
- Spicy Mini Chocolate Eclairs
- Popcorn à la Flinthart

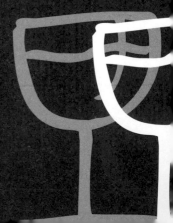

4. JUST THE two of us

When you are in a relationship, it's tempting to slip into DIY mode. This is because, after fighting your way to the office, fighting your way through the day, then fighting your way home again, you understandably want to do nothing. And, thankfully, once your intended has officially agreed to be yours, you no longer need to impress her. The fair lady is won, so the knight can put his feet up. He's fed her into submission. Now she can survive on ready meals, toast and takeaways like the rest of the kingdom. If she's after a banquet, she can do it herself! You go out to eat once a week, that's got to be enough for her! She can't expect you to slave over the hob for her on a workday. If you truly believe this nonsense, then you are a fool. The fair lady is only won for as long as the knight remains chivalrous.

And chivalrous means peeling your bottom off the sofa once in a while and getting your butt into the kitchen. We understand. You're dog-tired, you want to flop. The good news is, cooking *is* relaxing, especially when the recipes are as speedy and as simple as the ones here. Making your darling dinner after work is the perfect way to wind down. She can chat to you while you prepare the food, or scoot off for a bath while you have some time to yourself. But you can't lose. She is exquisitely grateful – partly because she is sick to the stomach of stodgy margheritas and rude delivery boys – and will remain affectionate and angelic for the rest of the evening. *And* she'll do the clearing up. Lastly, any smart man knows if she's happy, he's happy.

All recipes serve 2.

VEGETABLE AND CHEESE FRITTATA

This hearty dish is more substantial than an omelette. Plus,
you can vary the herbs or use other cheeses, such as diced
Brie or Boursin, instead of the feta cheese.

PREPARATION TIME: **10 MINUTES**
COOKING TIME: **8–9 MINUTES**

- 225g/8oz asparagus spears
- 175g/6oz broccoli florets
- 2 tbsp olive oil
- 4 spring onions, chopped
- 6 sun-dried tomatoes in oil, drained and chopped
- 4 eggs, beaten
- 2 tbsp chopped parsley
- salt and freshly ground black pepper
- 125g/4oz feta cheese, crumbled

1 Cut the asparagus into 5cm (2in) lengths. Parboil with the
   broccoli for 2–3 minutes, then drain thoroughly. Heat the grill
   to hot.

2 Meanwhile, heat the oil in a 20cm (8in) frying pan. Add all
   the vegetables and sun-dried tomatoes, and cook, stirring
   continuously, for 2 minutes. Pour in the beaten eggs. Add the
   parsley and season with a little salt and freshly ground black
   pepper. Cook, stirring continuously, for 1 minute, then leave to
   cook undisturbed for a further 3–4 minutes until the bottom of
   the frittata is set and lightly browned. Sprinkle the cheese over
   the frittata, then place under the grill for 1–2 minutes to set
   and brown the top. Cut into wedges and serve at once.

HOW
TO
BE
HER
KITCHEN LOVE GOD

THAI GREEN CHICKEN CURRY

With this versatile dish, you can use beef, lamb or even seafood, instead of chicken. Mushrooms, tomatoes and peas can be added, too.

PREPARATION TIME: **10 MINUTES**
COOKING TIME: **25 MINUTES**

- 2 tbsp oil
- 450g/1lb boneless chicken breasts or thighs
- 1–2 red chillies, deseeded and cut into slivers
- ½ red pepper, sliced
- 250g/9oz tiny new potatoes
- 1 tbsp Thai green curry paste
- 1 x 400g/14oz can coconut milk
- salt and freshly ground black pepper
- handful of fresh coriander, chopped
- 4 spring onions, shredded
- lime wedges, to garnish

1 Heat the oil in a heavy-based frying pan, then add the chicken pieces and brown lightly. Now add the sliced chillies and pepper with the new potatoes and cook, stirring, for 1 minute.

2 Stir the Thai curry paste and the coconut milk into the pan and bring to the boil. Lower the heat, season and allow to simmer, covered for about 20 minutes, until the chicken and the potatoes are cooked and tender.

3 Sprinkle on the chopped coriander and the shredded spring onions and season to taste. Garnish with lime wedges and serve with Fragrant Rice (*see opposite*).

FRAGRANT RICE

This is a perfect accompaniment to the Thai Green Chicken Curry, and will add flavour and interest to other curry dishes.

PREPARATION TIME: **5–7 MINUTES**
COOKING TIME: **12 MINUTES**

- 250g/9oz Thai fragrant or basmati rice
- 2 tbsp oil
- 1 small onion, chopped
- ½ tsp ground turmeric
- ½ tsp ground coriander
- ¼ tsp ground cumin
- 300ml/½ pint coconut milk or chicken stock
- 1 cinnamon stick
- 2 cloves
- 1 bay leaf
- salt, to taste

1 Put the rice in a sieve and rinse thoroughly with cold, running water. Drain.

2 Heat the oil in a saucepan, add the onion and fry on a medium heat for 3 minutes to soften. Add the rice and the ground spices and cook for 2 minutes, then stir in the coconut milk or chicken stock and all of the remaining ingredients. Bring to the boil and stir. Cover the pan with a lid or tin foil and turn the heat to its lowest setting. Leave for 10 minutes, until the rice is tender and fluffy. Serve hot.

HOT CHILLI SPECIAL

If you need warming up, try this veggie recipe. It uses store-cupboard items so you don't have to spend ages in the supermarket after work, buying the ingredients.

PREPARATION TIME: **7–8 MINUTES**
COOKING TIME: **20 MINUTES**

- 2 tbsp extra virgin olive oil
- 2 medium onions, thinly sliced
- 1 clove garlic, thinly sliced
- 1 dried red chilli, deseeded and crumbled
- ½ tsp dried thyme, tarragon or oregano
- 400g/14oz can chick-peas or cannelloni beans, drained
- 200g/7oz tin chopped plum tomatoes, drained
- 2 tsp Worcester sauce
- parsley, to garnish

1 Heat the oil in a saucepan and cook the onions for 1–2 minutes, then add the garlic and cook for 2–3 minutes. Add chilli and herbs, mix well, then add chick-peas and tomatoes. Cook over a medium heat for about 15 minutes, until liquid is well reduced.

2 Stir in the Worcester sauce and serve with vegetables. Garnish with parsley.

FIELD MUSHROOMS WITH OREGANO AND PARMESAN SHAVINGS

Meaty mushrooms are accompanied by herbs and cheese to create a tasty, light meal. Serve with a salad.

PREPARATION TIME: **4 MINUTES**
COOKING TIME: **6 MINUTES**

- ½ tbsp extra virgin olive oil
- 15g/½ oz butter
- 150g/5oz large field mushrooms, sliced
- 50g/2oz wedge Parmesan
- 2 thick slices of crusty white bread
- salt and freshly ground black pepper
- 1 garlic clove, roughly chopped
- small bunch fresh oregano, chopped
- small bunch flat-leaf parsley, chopped

1 Heat the oil and butter in a large frying pan, add the mushrooms and sauté, stirring often, for 3–4 minutes. Slice large shavings from the Parmesan and set aside. Meanwhile, toast 2 slices of bread, until golden.

2 Season the mushrooms with salt and freshly ground black pepper, stir in the garlic, oregano and parsley (keeping some for the garnish), then sprinkle two-thirds of the Parmesan shavings on top. Cover and leave for a few minutes until the cheese melts. To serve, heap the mushrooms on the toast and garnish with the rest of the herbs and Parmesan shavings.

HOW TO BE HER KITCHEN LOVE GOD

SCALLOPS WITH ORANGES AND PANCETTA

Another stylish quickie, the seafood and pancetta in this recipe are uplifted by a zingy, citrus flavour.

PREPARATION TIME: **5 MINUTES**
COOKING TIME: **5 MINUTES**

- 1 small orange
- 75g/3oz green beans
- 25g/1oz thinly sliced pancetta
- 8 large scallops and 6 shells
- fresh basil leaves to garnish

1   Peel the orange, then holding it over a bowl to catch the juice, cut out each segment, leaving the membrane.

2   Pour boiling water from the kettle into a saucepan, add the beans and simmer for 3–5 minutes. Heat a frying pan, then tear the pancetta into strips and dry-fry for a few minutes.

3   Slice each scallop in half or thirds lengthways and add to the pancetta. Sauté for 2 more minutes, add the orange segments and warm through for 1 minute.

4   Meanwhile, warm the shells under a moderate grill. Divide the scallop mixture between the shells, garnish with the basil leaves and serve immediately with the beans.

HOW TO BE HER KITCHEN LOVE GOD

WARM CHICKEN WALDORF SALAD

This salad is great at any time, but particularly with chilled white wine in summer.

PREPARATION TIME: **20 MINUTES**

- 1 handful of seedless white grapes, halved
- 1 stick celery, sliced
- half a red apple, cored and cut into bite-sized pieces
- 25g/1oz pecan nuts, toasted and roughly chopped
- 2 tbsp Greek yogurt
- ½ tbsp fresh mint, chopped
- 1 tsp honey (*optional*)
- salt and black pepper
- 1 small cos lettuce, washed and broken into small pieces
- ½ tbsp extra virgin olive oil
- ½ tsp lemon juice
- 1 cooked chicken breast, cut into strips

Salads are really great things to know. You can serve salads at practically any time of the day, and better still since they're prepared well before the meal is served, you can have them standing by, to be produced with a flourish. They impress the hell out of the broads, who suspect that the closest most men get to a salad is cocktail onions and hot chips.

• • •

There's all kinds of salads – crisp vegetable salads, pasta salads, fruit salads, salads with meat, salads with chicken or fish. They're a wonderfully versatile and tasty range of dishes. Be creative. Try out new and interesting vegetables. Throw in the odd cooked ingredient. Display your own ingenuity and bask in the female admiration which comes your way.

(Extract from *How to be a Man* by John Birmingham and Dick Flinthart)

1 Mix together the grapes, celery, apple, nuts, yogurt, mint and honey, if using. Season to taste.

2 Divide the lettuce between the serving plates and dress with the olive oil and lemon juice. Top with the Waldorf mixture and scatter over the chicken strips.

SOLE WITH A TOMATO SALSA

Plain fish on its own doesn't always inspire the taste buds, but pep it up with a tangy salsa and you'll love every bite of it.

PREPARATION TIME: **15 MINUTES**
COOKING TIME: **5 MINUTES**

- 1 tbsp chopped parsley
- 1 tsp small capers
- 1 gherkin, diced
- 2 plum tomatoes, deseeded and diced
- salt and pepper
- 2 lemon soles, skinned and filleted
- 25g/1oz flour
- olive oil, for frying
- 25g/1oz butter
- few drops of Worcester sauce
- juice of half a lemon

1 Preheat the oven to 425°F/220°C/gas mark 7.

2 In a bowl, combine the parsley, capers, gherkin and tomatoes and set aside. Season the sole fillets, then dredge them in the flour.

3 In a frying pan, heat a little olive oil until it is very hot and fry the fillets on both sides until brown. Transfer to a shallow baking dish.

4 Melt the butter in a frying pan, then add the Worcester sauce and lemon juice. Pour mixture over fillets and bake for 5 minutes. Remove from the oven, place on plates and sprinkle with the tomato salsa.

PAPPARDELLE WITH BACON AND VEGETABLES

Give this pasta dish extra punch by adding basil oil – this is available from most Italian delicatessens.

PREPARATION TIME: **15 MINUTES**
COOKING TIME: **35 MINUTES**

- 1 small onion, thinly sliced
- half a celery stick, thinly sliced
- 25g/1oz butter
- 3 tomatoes, peeled and chopped
- 225g/8oz courgettes, sliced
- salt and ground black pepper
- 50g/2oz bacon
- pinch of dried oregano
- 1½ tbsp basil oil (available from Italian delicatessens)
- 175g/6oz pappardelle (or tagliatelle, which is thinner)
- flat-leaf parsley, to garnish

1 Brown the onion and celery in a saucepan with the butter. Add the tomatoes and courgettes, cover and simmer for 20 minutes on a low heat, adding salt and pepper to taste. Dice the bacon and mix it into the sauce. Sprinkle with oregano, stir in half a tablespoon of the basil oil and cook for 15 minutes with the lid off.

2 Meanwhile, boil the pasta in salted water until *al dente* and drain. To serve, put the pasta into a soup tureen or serving bowl, sprinkle with the remaining basil oil and cover with the bacon and vegetable sauce. Garnish with sprigs of parsley.

LAMB CUTLETS WITH THYME, TOMATOES AND FENNEL

This colourful stew is quicker to make than many. Fennel is rather strong, so you may prefer celery.

PREPARATION TIME: **25 MINUTES**
COOKING TIME: **1 HOUR**

- 1½ tbsp olive oil
- 6 trimmed lamb cutlets
- 1 onion, chopped
- 1 garlic clove, crushed
- 75ml/3fl oz dry white wine
- 1 x 400g/14oz can of chopped tomatoes
- 1 tbsp chopped fresh thyme or ½ tbsp dried thyme
- 1 fennel bulb, cut into wedges
- salt and freshly ground black pepper
- 2 small tomatoes, quartered
- torn parsley or basil, to garnish

1 Heat the oil in a large, shallow saucepan. Fry the cutlets in batches quickly to brown all over. Set aside.

2 Add the onion and garlic and cook gently for 5 minutes. Return the cutlets to the pan and pour over the wine and tinned tomatoes. Stir in the thyme and fennel and season. Cook, covered, for 1 hour, until the lamb is tender.

3 Towards the end of the cooking time, add the quartered tomatoes to the pan. Cook, uncovered, on a fairly high heat to reduce the sauce. Season to taste and serve garnished with freshly torn parsley or basil.

CHICKEN WITH MUSHROOMS AND TOMATOES

Casseroled meat always tastes deliciously tender, and this chicken dish is a doddle to prepare.

PREPARATION TIME: **8 MINUTES**
COOKING TIME: **30 MINUTES**

- 2 chicken portions
- ½ tbsp fresh parsley or basil, chopped
- 2 cloves garlic, crushed
- 125g/4oz mushrooms, sliced
- 200g/7oz tin chopped tomatoes
- 125ml/4fl oz chicken stock or water
- half a spring onion, sliced
- 15g/½ oz butter

1 Preheat the oven to 180°C/350°F/gas mark 4.

2 Lay the chicken portions in a single layer in a small casserole or baking dish. Sprinkle on the herbs, garlic and mushrooms. Add tomatoes in their juice, stock or water, then top with the spring onion and dot with butter. Cover and cook in the oven for 30 minutes.

3 Perfect accompaniments are saffron rice (boiled rice with a teaspoon of saffron added to the water) and a selection of lightly cooked seasonal vegetables.

MANGO COULIS

You don't have to spend hours making a dessert. Just liven up your favourite ice cream or sorbet with this fruity sauce.

PREPARATION TIME: **5 MINUTES**

- 2 ripe mangoes
- juice of ½ lime or
  2 tbsp orange juice
- 2 tsp honey

1 Peel the mangoes and cut the flesh from the stone. Purée in a food processor with the lime juice and honey until smooth. Chill and serve cold.

SPICY MINI CHOCOLATE ECLAIRS

Give yourselves a midweek treat with these clever little eclairs made using shop-bought croissants.

PREPARATION TIME: **5 MINUTES**
COOKING TIME: **5 MINUTES**

- 50g/2oz plain chocolate, broken in pieces
- 3 lumps stem ginger in syrup, chopped
- 150ml/5fl oz crème fraîche
- 4 mini flaky croissants

1 Half fill a small saucepan with boiling water from the kettle and place over a medium heat. Melt the chocolate in a heatproof bowl over the saucepan. Mix three-quarters of the ginger into the crème fraîche. Halve the croissants and warm through under the grill.

2 Take them out and drizzle melted chocolate inside each warm croissant half. Spoon ginger crème fraîche on the bottom half, sandwich with the tops and drizzle over the remaining chocolate. Put 2 croissants on each plate and scatter the remaining ginger around the edge.

DANGER!
POPCORN À LA FLINTHART!

- 1 tbsp of garlic oil (made the same way as for the steak – see *page 42*)
- 175g/6oz popping corn per two people
- 1 dsp salt
- 2 dsp chicken stock
- 1 tbsp butter
- grated Parmesan cheese, to serve

1 In your stockpot, heat the garlic oil until a single kernel of popcorn in the bottom of the pan begins to spin around. At this point, add the rest of your popcorn, close the lid, and agitate the pan until the popping dies away. Pour the popcorn into a big salad bowl.

2 Cheat like crazy: mix a dessertspoon of salt and a dessertspoon of chicken stock and sprinkle the lot over the popcorn. Meanwhile melt a tablespoon of butter in the pan, and pour it over the popcorn. Toss the lot lightly, and sprinkle with grated Parmesan cheese.

(Extract from *How to be a Man* by John Birmingham and Dick Flinthart)

Roasted Parma Ham and Tomatoes

Tiger-tail Prawns and Puréed Red Pepper Sauce

Moroccan Chicken with Olives

Spring Leaf and Fruit Salad with Toasted Seeds

Saffron Mash

Tender Beef Stew with Orange and Mustard

Seed Topping

Baked Sea Bass

Roast Leg of Lamb with Creamy Onion Sauce

Roast Vegetables

Aubergine Steaks with Fresh Coriander

Turkey Breast with Herb Butter

and Wine Gravy

Sumptuous Bread and

Butter Pudding

5. COOKING
for the in-laws

Just plonk some leftovers in front of them, they won't mind. Ah ha ha ha. We all know the immeasurable importance of impressing the in-laws and their famed reluctance to be impressed. Especially by the man who is bonking their baby girl. But don't cry. It is possible to win them over with a super sumptuous meal. Sensational cooking speaks louder than words. It shows them you're not the abject loser they thought you were. It shows them you are capable of taking care of their darling daughter. It shows them that maybe she has chosen wisely after all. Admittedly, for these conclusions to be drawn, precautions are essential. First, check that Mummy and Daddy are not allergic to or disgusted by certain foodstuffs.

MAIN COURSES

The main course is the big number. You WILL be judged by this sample of cooking – so it's worth getting it spot on. You can either make them a real production number, like a major Thai stir-fry or Indian curry, or you can make them deceptively simple, and surround them with nifty salads and side-dishes. Remember, this is a showpiece meal, and you're cooking it with a purpose in mind, so take extra care and don't forget the value of presentation. A little patter about authenticity of recipes, cooking techniques, freshness of ingredients, personal touches, and good nutritional qualities is also helpful. Do some research before-hand. Also, try to pick a wine that will complement your meal rather than clash with it.

(Extract from *How to be a Man* by John Birmingham and Dick Flinthart)

Are they vegetarian? Vegan? Kosher? Do they hate fish or mushrooms or garlic or eggs? Ask before you plan, otherwise a rogue dislike will ruin your menu.

Presentation is also essential. Fork out on the serviettes, a vase of flowers, a good bottle of wine (but go easy on the booze or they will suspect you're an alcoholic) and ensure the cutlery sparkles. Her mother will probably prowl your flat in search of dust, defects and debauchery so keep the kitchen pristine and choke the toilet with scented bleach. Incidentally, not all mother-in-laws are talented chefs, but this won't stop them criticising. Velvet dagger remarks such as 'This is almost as good as my roast dinner!' or 'Not bad!' should be accepted graciously rather than picked over. Don't expect praise from Daddy. Be thankful he turned up.

This is, of course, the very worst case scenario. Chances are, her parents are charming, warm, friendly people who are touched at your invitation, thrilled to meet you and ecstatic that your arms don't trail along the floor. That you're a whizz in the kitchen is an overwhelming extra. Still, best to keep you on your toes.

All recipes serve 4.

HOW TO BE HER KITCHEN LOVE GOD

ROASTED PARMA HAM AND TOMATOES

Serve this dish as a tantalising starter and you will have your guests dishing out compliments well before the main course is served.

PREPARATION TIME: **15 MINUTES**
COOKING TIME: **25 MINUTES**

- 12 slices Parma ham
- 8 small tomatoes (or 4 large, halved)
- juice of 1 lime
- 2 tbsp olive oil
- sea salt, freshly ground black pepper
- 200g/7oz sugar snap peas
- 50g bag mixed salad leaves
- 30g/1½ oz Parmesan cheese, thinly sliced
- pinch golden caster sugar

1 Preheat oven to 180°C/350°F/gas mark 4. Arrange the Parma ham and tomatoes in an ovenproof dish, then drizzle over the lime juice, oil and seasoning. Bake until the tomatoes are cooked and the Parma ham is crispy.

2 Meanwhile, bring a large pan of water to the boil and blanch the sugar snap peas for a couple of minutes, then drain. Divide the peas and mixed leaves between four plates. Top with crispy ham, tomatoes and Parmesan. Add a pinch of sugar to the juices in the roasting pan, season well and drizzle over the salads.

TIGER-TAIL PRAWNS WITH PURÉED RED PEPPER SAUCE

The grilled and puréed peppers make a smoky-sweet sauce that's a perfect foil to the shellfish. Serve this as a starter or with rice, pasta or noodles, as a main course.

PREPARATION TIME: **15 MINUTES**
COOKING TIME: **20 MINUTES, APPROX.**

- 2 large red peppers
- 1 tsp olive oil
- 1 clove garlic, crushed
- good pinch of dried chilli flakes
- 450g/1lb uncooked tiger-tail prawns, shells removed
- salt and freshly ground black pepper
- shredded spring onion, to garnish

1 Preheat the grill to hot. Halve the peppers lengthways and remove the seeds. Place, skin side up, under the grill. Cook for 10–15 minutes until the skins are blackened and blistered. Cool slightly, then peel and discard the skins. Roughly chop the peppers and purée, using a blender or food processor.

2 Heat the olive oil in a large frying pan. Add the garlic and chilli flakes and cook over a medium heat for a few seconds, then stir in the prawns. Cook until the prawn flesh is firm and opaque, then remove to a serving dish or individual plates. Keep hot.

3 Add the pepper purée to the pan and heat through, stirring. Add a little water, if necessary, to give a thick sauce. Season to taste and serve at once with the prawns, garnished with a little shredded spring onion.

HOW TO BE HER KITCHEN LOVE GOD

MOROCCAN CHICKEN WITH OLIVES

Start marinating the chicken the night before, so it is full of exotic flavour when you serve it up.

PREPARATION TIME: **15 MINUTES (PLUS 8 HOURS MARINATING)**
COOKING TIME: **40 MINUTES**

- ½ red chilli, deseeded and diced
- ½ dried red chilli, crushed
- 3 cloves garlic, chopped
- 1 cinnamon stick, split in half
- ¼ tsp paprika
- 1 tsp ground toasted cumin seeds
- pinch of saffron threads or ½ tsp of turmeric
- juice of half an orange
- 3 tbsp olive oil
- 4 skinless chicken breasts
- 2 Spanish onions, sliced
- 50g/2oz green olives, stoned
- 50g/2oz black olives, stoned
- 100ml/4fl oz chicken stock
- 8 tomatoes, deseeded and diced
- 100g/4oz green beans
- 2 tbsp fresh mint

1 In the morning, or the night before, mix the chillies, garlic, cinnamon, paprika, cumin, saffron or turmeric, orange juice and 1½ tbsp olive oil. Put the chicken in a dish, spoon over the marinade, cover the dish, refrigerate and leave to marinate.

2 Before your guests arrive, prepare the remaining ingredients. Fry the onions in the rest of the olive oil over a medium heat for 15 minutes until golden, then put to one side. 30 minutes before eating, add the chicken to the onions and sear over a high heat until brown (about 2 minutes each side). Add the marinade, olives and the stock and simmer for 15 minutes.

3 Remove the chicken and leave to rest. Add the tomatoes, green beans and mint to the sauce and reduce by boiling rapidly for 5 minutes. Remove the cinnamon. Slice the chicken in diagonal pieces. Serve with Saffron Mash (*see page 101*), spooning the sauce around the mash. Garnish with fresh mint.

HOW
TO
BE
HER
KITCHEN LOVE GOD

SPRING LEAF AND FRUIT SALAD WITH TOASTED SEEDS

This fruity, perky salad is ideal for freshening the taste buds, especially if you're planning to have a rich main course.

PREPARATION TIME: **12 MINUTES**

- 5 tbsp pumpkin seeds
- 3 tbsp sunflower seeds
- 1 large bowl mixed salad leaves, torn if large
- 4 oranges, peeled and thinly sliced
- 1 small bunch seedless grapes
- salt and freshly ground black pepper
- mayonnaise, to serve

1 Sprinkle the seeds onto a baking sheet and toast under a hot grill until lightly golden. They may pop a little, so take care as you remove them from the grill. Allow to cool.

2 Put the remaining ingredients into a serving bowl and season. Toss together lightly, scatter over the toasted seeds and drizzle with mayonnaise.

HOW
TO
BE
HER
KITCHEN LOVE GOD

SAFFRON MASH

These creamy, smooth mashed potatoes, coloured with saffron, are the ideal accompaniment to the Moroccan Chicken dish.

PREPARATION TIME: **30 MINUTES**
COOKING TIME: **30 MINUTES**

- 900g/2 lb floury potatoes
- 500ml/1 pint chicken stock
- pinch sea salt
- pinch saffron threads
- 1 clove garlic, chopped
- 150ml/5fl oz milk
- 75ml/3fl oz extra virgin olive oil
- pinch paprika

1 Peel and cube the potatoes and put in a saucepan with the stock and salt. Cover the potatoes with water and bring to the boil.

2 Put the saffron, garlic and milk into a different saucepan and bring to the boil. Cover and remove from the heat. When cooked, drain and mash the potatoes, stirring in the milk slowly. Add the oil and paprika and season to taste. Keep the mash warm in a low oven until ready to serve.

HOW TO BE HER KITCHEN LOVE GOD

TENDER BEEF STEW WITH ORANGE AND MUSTARD SEED TOPPING

Stewing is a deliciously lazy way to cook. Whilst this dish is left to simmer away, you can get on with a last-minute tidy before the guests arrive.

PREPARATION TIME: **30 MINUTES**
COOKING TIME: **2 HOURS, APPROX.**

- 3 tbsp olive oil
- 700g/1½ lb stewing beef, cubed
- 1 onion, chopped
- 12 whole baby onions or shallots
- 2 garlic cloves, chopped
- 1 tbsp flour
- 1 cinnamon stick, broken into two
- 150ml/5fl oz red wine
- 300ml/11fl oz beef stock
- 1 sprig fresh thyme or 1½ tsp dried thyme
- salt and freshly ground black pepper
- 225g/8oz button mushrooms

For the topping
- 1 garlic clove
- fresh parsley
- pared zest of 1 orange
- 2 tsp mustard seeds

1 Preheat the oven to 180°C/350°F/gas mark 4. Heat 1 tbsp oil in a large saucepan. On a high heat, add the beef and brown quickly on all sides. Transfer to a casserole dish.

HOW TO BE HER KITCHEN LOVE GOD

2 Add onion and baby onions or shallots to the saucepan. Cook on a medium heat for 8–10 minutes until soft and lightly browned. Stir in garlic and flour and cook for 1 minute. Add cinnamon, red wine, beef stock and thyme to the pan. Season with salt and pepper. Bring to the boil. Pour mixture over the meat, cover and cook in oven for about 2 hours. Just before serving, fry mushrooms in the remaining oil and stir into the beef. Make topping by chopping together the garlic and parsley. Mix with the orange rind and mustard seeds and scatter over meat.

HOW TO BE HER KITCHEN LOVE GOD

BAKED SEA BASS

If your in-laws are fish fans, then you'll make a real impression when you serve a whole fish with this fabulously fast main course.

PREPARATION TIME: **15 MINUTES**
COOKING TIME: **40 MINUTES, APPROX.**

- sea bass or other whole fish, weighing about 1.5kg/2½ lb, cleaned
- freshly ground black pepper
- 4 sprigs rosemary
- 1 sprig bay leaves
- 5 sprigs parsley
- 2 garlic cloves, chopped
- 3 tbsp olive oil
- 6 canned anchovy fillets, drained
- 40g/1½ oz stale white breadcrumbs
- 25g/1oz walnuts, very finely chopped
- lemon slices, herb sprigs and extra walnuts, to garnish

1 Preheat the oven to 180°C/350°F/gas mark 4. Lightly oil a baking dish or tin large enough to hold the whole fish, then rinse the fish and pat dry. Season the cavity with freshly ground black pepper.

2 Lay the sprigs of rosemary and bay leaves in the bottom of the baking tin and put the fish on top. Stuff the fish with the parsley and garlic.

HOW TO BE HER KITCHEN LOVE GOD

3 Heat the oil in a small pan. Add the anchovies and cook gently for a minute or two until dissolved, stirring with a fork to help break them up, then place on top of the fish. Mix together the breadcrumbs and chopped walnuts. Sprinkle on top of the anchovies and bake the fish in the oven for about 40 minutes, until it's cooked through and the flesh flakes easily.

4 Serve on a platter, garnished with lemon slices, herb sprigs and walnuts.

HOW
TO
BE
HER
KITCHEN LOVE GOD

ROAST LEG OF LAMB WITH CREAMY ONION SAUCE

A traditional roast is usually a safe bet and the rich, creamy sauce that accompanies this recipe is bound to bowl your guests over.

PREPARATION TIME: **40 MINUTES**
COOKING TIME: **1 HOUR 50 MINUTES**

- 1 leg of lamb, weighing about 1.5kg/3½ lb
- 1 tsp mustard powder or 2 tsp Dijon mustard
- salt and freshly ground black pepper
- 2 sprigs rosemary

Creamy onion sauce
- 2 small onions
- 25g/1oz butter
- 3 level tbsp flour
- 300ml/½ pint milk
- salt and freshly ground black pepper
- freshly grated nutmeg

Gravy
- 175ml/6fl oz port
- 100ml/3½ fl oz water
- 4 tbsp redcurrant jelly
- 1 tsp cornflour mixed with 2 tbsp cold water

1 Preheat the oven to 230°C/450°F/gas mark 8. Smear the lamb with the mustard, season and place in a roasting tin. Place one rosemary sprig underneath the lamb and one on top. Roast in the oven for 20 minutes, then lower the oven temperature to 180°C/350°F/gas mark 4 and cook for 1½ hours.

2 Meanwhile, prepare the onion sauce. Halve and slice the onions. Melt the butter in a saucepan and add the onions. Cook on a low heat for about 15 minutes until the onions are soft – don't let them brown. Add the flour and cook, stirring for 1 minute, then remove from the heat and gradually stir in the milk. Return the pan to the heat and bring to the boil and stir until thickened. Let the sauce bubble gently for 1 minute, then season and add nutmeg. Serve hot.

3 When the lamb is cooked, transfer it to a serving platter and leave it to rest for 15 minutes before carving. Discard the rosemary sprigs. Meanwhile, prepare the gravy. Pour off excess fat from the roasting tin and add the port and water to the tin. Bring to the boil and cook over a fairly high heat for two minutes, stirring and scraping up the sediment with a wooden spoon. Add the redcurrant jelly and stir until dissolved. Add the cornflour paste, stir until the gravy thickens, then let it bubble for 1 minute. Strain into a warm jug. Serve the lamb with the gravy, new potatoes, broad beans and onion sauce.

HOW TO BE HER KITCHEN LOVE GOD

ROAST VEGETABLES

These go well with fish and grilled or roast meat dishes, and are especially good served with a dollop of soured cream.

PREPARATION TIME: **20 MINUTES**
COOKING TIME: **40 MINUTES, APPROX.**

- 225g/8oz baby parsnips
- 225g/8oz smallish carrots
- 225g/8oz baby turnips
- 225g/8oz celeriac, diced
- 350g/12oz small, whole new potatoes
- 2 onions, quartered, with root end intact
- 100ml/4fl oz mixture of vegetable and olive oil
- 1 to 2 tsp caster sugar
- 1 level tsp ground allspice
- salt and freshly ground black pepper
- 3 sprigs rosemary

1 Preheat the oven to 200°C/400°F/gas mark 6. Bring a large pan of water to the boil. Cut the parsnips and carrots in half lengthways and trim the turnips. Add these and the celeriac to the pan and return to the boil, then strain into a colander.

2 Put the blanched vegetables, along with the new potatoes and the onions, into a large roasting dish. Drizzle over the oil mixture and sprinkle with the sugar, allspice and salt and pepper. Toss well to mix. Tuck the rosemary sprigs among the vegetables and roast in the oven, stirring occasionally, for about 40 minutes, until the vegetables are tender and browned. Serve hot.

AUBERGINE STEAKS WITH FRESH CORIANDER

Aubergine is a perfect companion for lamb, and this recipe has the delicious added flavour of coriander.

PREPARATION TIME: **10 MINUTES**
COOKING TIME: **40 MINUTES**

- 3 large aubergines
- 4 cloves garlic (skin on)
- olive oil
- handful fresh coriander leaves
- freshly ground black pepper
- 2 lemons, cut into wedges

1 Preheat the oven to 200°C/400°F/gas mark 6. Slice the aubergines in half, lengthways and widthways. Make half a dozen deep diagonal slashes across each flat side, almost cutting through. Repeat at the opposite angle to give a diamond effect.

2 Put the aubergine pieces skin-side down in a roasting tin with the garlic, sprinkle all over with oil and bake for 40 minutes. They should be soft to the touch, but still have their shape.

3 Scatter with coriander and serve with freshly ground black pepper and lemon wedges.

HOW TO BE HER KITCHEN LOVE GOD

TURKEY BREAST WITH HERB BUTTER AND WINE GRAVY

Turkey doesn't need to be served just at Christmas. However, if you are entertaining your in-laws during the seasonal festivities, then this is a speedy alternative to the classic roast theme.

PREPARATION TIME: **30 MINUTES**
COOKING TIME: **45 MINUTES**

- handful of fresh herbs (parsley, tarragon, thyme, sage or a mixture) finely chopped
- around 125g/4oz butter, softened
- salt and freshly ground black pepper
- 4 skinless, boneless turkey fillets
- 8 rashers of streaky bacon, rind removed
- 4 medium carrots, peeled and thinly sliced
- 4 medium onions, peeled and thinly sliced
- 4 stalks of celery, thinly sliced
- 350ml/12fl oz dry white wine or vermouth
- 350ml/12fl oz chicken stock (from a cube)
- tray of shop-bought stuffing
- 450g/1lb potatoes, peeled and quartered
- 450g/1lb Brussels sprouts
- 2 tbsp flour

1 Preheat the oven to 230°C/450°F/gas mark 8. Mix the herbs with the butter and season with salt and pepper. Cut a deep pocket into the thickest side of the turkey fillet and stuff with the butter mixture. Wrap two bacon rashers around each fillet and secure with a toothpick.

2 Put the vegetables in a roasting tin with the turkey fillets on top. Pour in a large splash of wine or vermouth, a large splash of stock and a large splash of water (to prevent the butter burning). Put the roasting tin on the middle shelf of the oven. Place the tray of stuffing on the shelf below. Put the potatoes in a tin containing ½in preheated oil and place on the shelf above the turkey.

3 Cook for about 45 minutes, until the meat juices run clear when pricked with a skewer or sharp knife. Baste three or four times with the juices during cooking, and add more water if the pan is drying out.

4 Place the Brussels sprouts into a saucepan of salted, boiling water 15 minutes before serving.

5 About 10 minutes before serving, transfer the turkey fillets to a serving dish and cover them loosely with tin foil. Place the roasting tin over a low heat and, when the juices start to sizzle, make the gravy by sprinkling the flour over the juices and vegetables. Stir well for 1–2 minutes, scraping the bottom of the pan to dislodge the tasty, cooked-on bits. Pour in the remaining wine and stock and cook, stirring regularly, until the liquid is thick enough to coat the back of a spoon (around 3–5 minutes).

6 To serve, put the drained vegetables, stuffing and gravy in serving dishes. Uncover the turkey, slice and serve with cranberry sauce.

SUMPTUOUS BREAD AND BUTTER PUDDING

Traditional British grub seems to be making a welcome return and this luxurious pudding is sure to go down a treat with Mum and Dad.

PREPARATION TIME: **10 MINUTES (PLUS 15 MINUTES RESTING)**
COOKING TIME: **1 HOUR, APPROX.**

- 50g/2oz softened butter
- 8–10 slices good white bread
- large handful raisins or sultanas
- 2 tsp powdered cinnamon
- 6 eggs, beaten
- 1.5 litres/2½ pints semi-skimmed milk
- 5–8 tbsp brown sugar
- cream (single or double) or crème fraîche, to serve

1   Butter the bread generously, then put one layer in a large shallow baking dish. Sprinkle over the raisins or sultanas and cinnamon, then top with the remaining bread, buttered side up. Mix the eggs with the milk and half the sugar, then pour over the bread. Leave to sit for 15 minutes. If left longer, cover and refrigerate.

2   Preheat the oven to 180°C/350°F/gas mark 4. Sprinkle the remaining sugar over the pudding and bake in the middle of the oven for around 1 hour until a knife inserted in the centre of the pudding comes out clean and hot. Serve with the cream or crème fraîche.

- Honey Soy Sausages with Wholegrain Mustard
- Chilli and Coriander Prawns
- Home-spiced Popcorn
- Sizzling Salsa
- Serious Bad-Ass Guacamole
- Chicken Burritos
- The Great American Hamburger
- Spicy Burgers
- Hot Tomato Relish
- Sweet Potato Wedges with Crispy Paprika Onions
- Oven Fries
- Cucumber and Coriander Raita
- Quick Chicken Curry
- Linguine with Crumbled Sausage and Spinach
- Mr Flinthart's Infamous Mr Monster Pancakes

6. NIGHT IN
with the lads

The pressure is off! You cannot fail to impress people who have, at some point in their lives, survived on economy sausages and Ginster's pork pies. Most men go through a stage of eating badly. It becomes a competition. Some favour an exclusive diet of kebabs, smoky bacon crisps and KFC. Others forge toasted cheese sandwiches with the iron. Some prefer the nutritious twosome of beer and cigarettes. An unfortunate few – such as my husband – let their college friends cater for them and were rewarded with chips fried in castor oil. But that was then. You were all pipsqueaks. Now you are grown-ups, with jobs, cars, bills and girlfriends. You may have even visited the theatre once or twice. I'm teasing. Point is, you are all infinitely more refined, you don't want to die young, thus your culinary standards have rocketed.

So the pressure's on again. But it's a relatively low heat. At least you can shut your pals in the lounge with some beers and a PlayStation and know you'll be left alone to create. And, despite the lads' graduation to sophistication, until you build up an inevitable reputation for fabulous cooking, their expectations will be delightfully reasonable. Less joyfully, it's almost certain that not one of them will offer to help clear up, so it's best to tidy up as you go. Alternatively, you could take a stand. It's infuriating that the most modern of men rudely rock back on their chairs and fiddle with the stem of their wine glass while women feel obliged to collect the dirty plates and plod towards the sink. So if you force your pals into the kitchen to wash up – congratulations – you'll be doing us all a favour.

HONEY SOY SAUSAGES WITH WHOLEGRAIN MUSTARD

Keep your mates happy with these saucy dippers while you play the perfect host and dish out the beers.

SERVES: **6**
PREPARATION TIME: **10 MINUTES (PLUS 20 MINUTES MARINATING)**
COOKING TIME: **25–30 MINUTES**

- 3 tbsp honey
- 2 tbsp soy sauce
- 3 tbsp wholegrain mustard
- 6 cloves of garlic, peeled
- 30 cocktail sausages

For the mustard dip
- 4 tbsp wholegrain mustard
- 3 tbsp natural yogurt
- 1 clove of garlic, peeled and crushed

1 Preheat the oven to 200°C/400°F/gas mark 6. Place the honey, soy sauce, mustard and garlic in a bowl, mix well. Place the sausages on a baking tray and pour over the marinade, season well. Cover and leave for 20 minutes.

2 Place the baking tray in the oven and cook the sausages in the marinade for 25–30 minutes, turning occasionally. Now prepare the mustard dip by mixing the ingredients together. Serve the sausages with the dip and plenty of napkins!

HOW TO BE HER KITCHEN LOVE GOD

CHILLI AND CORIANDER PRAWNS

Make this starter well before your guests arrive, as you need to marinate the prawns to give them their delicious Eastern flavour.

SERVES: **5**
MAKES: **10**
PREPARATION TIME: **10 MINUTES PLUS 1 HOUR MARINATING**

- finely grated rind of ½ lime
- ½ tbsp chilli oil (make your own with
  ½ tbsp olive oil and ¼ red chilli,
  deseeded and chopped)
- ½ tbsp freshly chopped coriander
- 50g/2oz cooked king prawns
- salt, freshly ground black pepper

1 Combine the lime, chilli oil and coriander, add the prawns and season. Leave to marinate for at least 1 hour. Serve on a platter with a dish of cocktail sticks.

HOME-SPICED POPCORN

These tasty, hot nibbles can be served up in minutes – they're healthy too, although that probably won't be of great concern to your mates!

SERVES **6**
PREPARATION TIME: **5 MINUTES**
COOKING TIME: **1 MINUTE**

- 4 tbsp olive oil
- 1 red chilli, deseeded and chopped
- 3 tsp English Provender Very Lazy Garlic
  (available from supermarkets)
- 225g/8oz popping corn
- ½ tsp each chilli powder, sea salt
  and cayenne pepper

1 Heat half the oil with half the chilli and garlic in the largest heavy-based saucepan you can find. Add half the popcorn, chilli powder, salt and cayenne pepper and toss together to coat the popcorn. Cover the saucepan and cook over a high heat, shaking the pan continuously to prevent the popcorn from burning, until all of it has popped (about 1 minute). Repeat with the remaining ingredients.

2 Serve the popcorn in one large bowl.

HOW
TO
BE
HER
KITCHEN LOVE GOD

SIZZLING SALSA

This classic quickie is easy to make and excellent with grilled steak, tortilla chips and Mexican dishes.

SERVES: **4–6**

PREPARATION TIME: **12 MINUTES (PLUS 2 HOURS STANDING)**

- 1 mild onion, chopped
- 1 celery stick, finely chopped
- 4 large ripe tomatoes, skinned, deseeded and chopped
- 1 inch piece of fresh root ginger, grated
- 4 fresh medium red chillies, finely chopped
- ½–1 tsp crushed dried chilli flakes
- 2 tbsp fresh coriander, chopped
- 1 tbsp lime juice
- salt and freshly ground black pepper

1 Mix together all the ingredients, except the seasoning, in a bowl. Use a food processor if you have one, but make sure the mixture doesn't get too mushy. Season with salt and freshly ground black pepper, to taste. Cover and leave to stand for at least 2 hours to allow the flavours to mingle. Serve at room temperature.

HOW TO BE HER KITCHEN LOVE GOD

SERIOUS BAD-ASS GUACAMOLE

- 2 rashers of bacon, diced
- 1 medium onion, diced
- 1 tsp garlic, chopped
- 2 ripe avocadoes
- 1 large tomato, diced
- 1 red pepper, diced finely
- 250ml tub sour cream
- 1 tbsp fresh black pepper
- juice of 2 limes

1 Fry the bacon until it's crisp, and put it in a salad bowl. Use the bacon grease to fry the onion and garlic briefly – just until the onion begins to turn clear – and toss them into the salad bowl too.

2 Mush the avocadoes into a smooth pulp with the bacon and onion and garlic, and stir in the tomato and the pepper. Stir in the sour cream, the black pepper and the lime juice. Add a dash of cumin powder too, if you like. Serve with super fresh bread, or better still, plain tortilla chips.

(Extract from *How to be a Man* by John Birmingham and Dick Flinthart)

HOW TO BE HER KITCHEN LOVE GOD

CHICKEN BURRITOS

Get your mates to do a bit of work by having them tuck into some great DIY food. Serve up the ingredients in separate bowls.

SERVES: **8**
PREPARATION TIME: **10 MINUTES**

- 8 floured tortillas, heated through
- 150ml/5fl oz natural yogurt
- chilli oil
- 3 ready-cooked Mexican chicken breasts (from supermarkets), shredded
- 1 red onion, peeled and shredded
- 1 avocado, peeled and diced
- 2 plum tomatoes, skinned, seeded and chopped

1 Take one warmed tortilla and spread with yogurt, then a drizzling of chilli oil. Top with a little shredded chicken, and the vegetables. Roll up tightly and cut through the middle. Drizzle with a little extra chilli oil, if you wish.

HOW TO BE HER KITCHEN LOVE GOD

THE GREAT AMERICAN HAMBURGER

Burgers may be a favourite fast food, but these home-made ones, made with good quality mince, will give you something to really sink your teeth into.

SERVES: **4**
PREPARATION TIME: **10 MINUTES**
COOKING TIME: **UP TO 15 MINUTES**

- 600g/1½ lb good mince beef
- salt, to season
- 1 tbsp vegetable oil (*optional*)
- 4 thin slices Cheddar or Gruyère cheese (*optional*)
- 4 large hamburger buns
- fried onions, slices of fresh tomato and ketchup, to serve

1 Form the beef into patties, about 2cm (¾ inch) thick, then preheat the grill or a heavy frying pan until medium-hot. Season the burgers with salt and add to the pan. You don't need to use the oil if the pan is non-stick. Cook, without moving them, until they are well browned, with a good crust (3–4 minutes), then turn them over and cook the other side (5–7 minutes for rare, 8–10 minutes for medium-rare, an extra minute for medium).

2 In the final 2 minutes of cooking, lay a cheese slice over each burger and, if you're frying, cover the pan. Serve the burgers in the buns with fried onions, slices of fresh tomato, ketchup and Hot Tomato Relish, with Oven Fries on the side (*see pages 125 and 128*).

HOW TO BE HER KITCHEN LOVE GOD

SPICY BURGERS

**The curry butter filling makes this a great alternative
to the traditional burger and provides added bite.**

SERVES: **4**
PREPARATION TIME: **12 MINUTES**
COOKING TIME: **10 MINUTES, APPROX.**

- 400g/14oz minced beef
- 1 onion, chopped
- 50g/2oz butter
- 2 tbsp curry powder
- 1 tsp lemon juice
- 125g/4oz bacon
- 2 tbsp oil
- ½ onion
- 4 hamburger buns or baps
- 25g/1oz Leerdammer cheese
- fresh rosemary leaves (*optional*)

1 First make the hamburgers by kneading the minced beef with
   the chopped onion, and dividing into patties. Then beat the
   butter until very soft and add the curry powder and the lemon
   juice. Cook the hamburgers under the grill for about 5 minutes
   on each side, or less if you prefer them rare.

2 Cut the bacon into small pieces and brown in a frying pan with
   the oil. Slice the onion into rings. Cut the roll in half, spread on
   the curry butter. Add the hamburgers, bacon and onion.

3 To serve, sprinkle with grated Leerdammer and garnish with
   fresh rosemary leaves.

HOT TOMATO RELISH

The hot, tangy flavour of this spicy relish goes well with both of the burger recipes.

PREPARATION TIME: **12 MINUTES (PLUS 1 HOUR STANDING)**

- 2 ripe tomatoes
- 1 thin slice of onion
- 1 small red chilli
- 1 red pepper
- 1 tsp sugar
- 1 tsp red wine vinegar
- salt and black pepper, to season

1 Halve the tomatoes, scoop out the seeds and cut the flesh into small chunks. Chop the onion finely. Deseed the chilli and chop finely. Then deseed the red pepper and cut into small chunks. Mix the ingredients in a ceramic or glass bowl with the sugar and vinegar. Season with salt and pepper and leave for an hour, tossing occasionally, to let the flavours blend.

HOW TO BE HER KITCHEN LOVE GOD

SWEET POTATO WEDGES WITH CRISPY PAPRIKA ONIONS

If you don't want chips with everything then try these. The natural sugar in sweet potatoes melts to a wonderful sticky caramel when oven-baked.

SERVES: **4**
PREPARATION TIME: **15 MINUTES**
COOKING TIME: **30 MINUTES**

- 4–6 sweet potatoes, washed
- 50g/2oz butter, melted
- 75ml/3fl oz olive oil
- sea salt
- handful fresh coriander leaves
- 4 large Spanish onions, finely sliced
- ½ tsp paprika
- 50g/2oz pistachio nuts
- 2 tbsp Greek yogurt
- 2 tbsp mayonnaise
- small handful fresh mint leaves

1 Preheat the oven to 220°C/425°F/gas mark 7. Cut the potatoes in half lengthways, then cut each half into wedges and put into a bowl. Pour half the butter and oil over the wedges, toss well to coat. Arrange the wedges in a single layer on two baking sheets, season with sea salt and scatter over half the coriander leaves. Bake for 8–10 minutes. Turn the slices over and bake for another 7 minutes or until crisp on the outside and soft in the middle.

2 Meanwhile, heat the remaining oil and butter in a large frying pan and fry the onion with the paprika over a medium heat until crisp, approximately 10 minutes. Dry-fry the pistachio nuts for a couple of minutes and roughly chop. Add the remaining coriander and toasted pistachio to the onion and toss everything together.

3 Mix yogurt and mayonnaise together. Divide the potato chunks between warm shallow bowls, spoon the crispy onion mixture on top, followed by the mayonnaise mixture. Scatter over fresh mint leaves and serve with courgettes and sugar snap peas.

OVEN FRIES

You don't need to worry about a deep-fat fryer to cook up these delicious fries that will round off your burger meal.

PREPARATION TIME: **7 MINUTES**
COOKING TIME: **30 MINUTES, APPROX.**

- 2 large baking potatoes
- 5 tbsp vegetable oil
- salt

1 Preheat the oven to 200°C/400°F/Gas Mark 6. Peel the potatoes, if you like, then cut into 1.5cm (½ inch) slices. Halve each slice and dry well on a piece of kitchen roll. Brush both sides with oil and lay on one or two large baking sheets. Sprinkle with salt and bake near the top of the oven, turning once, until they are well-browned on the outside and cooked through (about 30 minutes).

HOW TO BE HER KITCHEN LOVE GOD

CUCUMBER AND CORIANDER RAITA

Cool down your curry (*overleaf*) with this refreshing, traditional Indian accompaniment.

PREPARATION TIME: **10 MINUTES**

- 7cm (3 inch) length of cucumber
- 225ml/8fl oz low-fat natural yogurt
- small handful of fresh coriander, coarsely chopped
- salt and freshly ground black pepper

1 Halve the cucumber lengthways and remove the seeds. Slice, then pat dry with kitchen roll or a clean towel. Whisk the yogurt and mix in the cucumber and coriander.

2 Season, then leave for 5 minutes for flavours to blend before serving.

HOW TO BE HER KITCHEN LOVE GOD

QUICK CHICKEN CURRY

This is sure to bring back fond memories of staggering from the pub to the curry house. Use a good curry powder, such as Pataks.

SERVES: **4**
PREPARATION TIME: **25 MINUTES**
COOKING TIME: **25–35 MINUTES, APPROX.**

- 2 tbsp vegetable oil
- 1 clove of garlic, finely chopped
- 2.5cm (1 inch) piece of fresh ginger, finely chopped
- 1 large onion, finely chopped
- 1 bay leaf
- 1 green chilli, deseeded and finely chopped, or ½–1 tsp chilli powder
- 4 chicken pieces (breast or leg)
- 1–2 tsp medium curry powder or garam masala
- 300ml/10fl oz water
- small handful of raisins or sultanas (*optional*)
- half a chicken stock cube (*optional*)

1   Heat the oil in a casserole or a large, heavy frying pan with a lid. Add garlic, ginger, onion, bay leaf and chilli to taste. Fry, stirring frequently, until the mixture starts to turn golden (around 5–10 minutes). Add more chilli, if necessary.

2 Meanwhile, set the grill on high and cook the chicken on both sides until lightly browned (around 3 minutes each side). Add to the pot, with the curry powder or garam masala, and fry for one minute, adding a little water if the mixture starts to stick to the bottom of the pan.

3 Add the water and the raisins or sultanas, if using. You can also add the half chicken stock cube for extra flavour. Bring to the boil, then reduce the heat and cover. Simmer for 25–35 minutes, depending on how well you like your chicken cooked.

4 Serve immediately, accompanied by rice (cooked with ½ tsp of turmeric for colour), Cucumber and Coriander Raita (*see page 129*), green vegetables and a selection of ready-made chutneys and relishes.

HOW TO BE HER

KITCHEN LOVE GOD

LINGUINE WITH CRUMBLED SAUSAGE AND SPINACH

Fill 'em up with a meaty pasta dish that will only have you slaving in the kitchen for a few minutes.

SERVES: **4**
PREPARATION TIME: **2 MINUTES**
COOKING TIME: **8 MINUTES**

- 1 packet fresh linguine or tagliatelle
- 1 tbsp olive oil
- 4 good quality pork and herb sausages, skinned
- 2 tsp crushed or puréed garlic
- pinch of chilli flakes
- 2 tbsp tomato purée
- 1 glass of white wine
- 75g/3oz fresh spinach leaves

1 Cook the pasta in a large pan of boiling water until firm to the bite.

2 Meanwhile, heat the oil in a large frying pan. Crumble the sausage meat into the pan with the garlic, chilli flakes and tomato purée. Cook over a medium heat for 5 minutes, breaking up the meat with a fork. Add the wine and spinach and cook on a high heat for 3 more minutes. To serve, drain the pasta, stir it into the sausage mixture and spoon onto plates.

REAL HANGOVER FOOD
MR. FLINTHART'S INFAMOUS
MR. MONSTER PANCAKES

These beasties are easy to make, cheap, delicious, and very filling – just the thing if you decide to feed 20 or 30 people the morning after a really big one. For each person you will need:

- 140g/5oz self-raising flour
- 1 egg
- 1 tbsp of icing sugar
- 100ml/3½ fl oz of milk
  vanilla essence

1 Whisk the whole lot together into a thick batter, adding a dash of vanilla essence. In a frying pan set over a medium heat, melt a pat of butter, and ladle in the batter. About 1½ ladles will turn out a very serious pancake.

2 Let the batter cook until the edges look doughy, and you can see bubble-craters in the middle. Initially, you'll need to carefully turn the pancakes with your spatula so they can toast on the other side for about 20 seconds – but when you get better at it, a simple, arrogant flick of the wrist will turn the things over in the pan and make you look like a complete Kitchen Samurai.

3 Serve hot, with butter and real maple syrup. And tequila!

(Extract from *How to be a Man* by John Birmingham and Dick Flinthart)

- Smoked Salmon and Asparagus Salad
- Warm Pears with Blue Cheese and Walnuts
- Wild Rocket and Bacon Salad
- Cold Lobster with Chilli Mayonnaise
- Duck Breasts with Raspberry Vinegar
- Red Mullet, Mussel and Grilled Pepper Risotto with Saffron
- Stewed Lamb with Coriander and Toasted Almonds
- Salade Rosé
- Rich Chocolate Crème Brulée
- The Ultimate Chocolate Truffles
- Strawberries and Brazil Nuts with Chocolate Sauce

7. MAKE UP meals

You're starting with minus points. You need no reminder of the enormity of your task. But let's clarify the situation, anyway. You've had a humdinger of a row. You, obviously, were at fault otherwise you wouldn't feel obliged to make it up to her with a fancy meal. So when we say fancy, we're talking high church fancy. We're talking Liberace on his birthday. We're talking Cruella DeVil at the Christmas party. We're talking the full works, all the trimmings, no expense or cliché spared. Because that, I'm very much afraid, is what it's going to take. Your woman is not a sadist but she wants to see you grovel. And a sorry bunch of primary coloured blooms from Texaco won't swing it. You were going to the garage anyway to buy cigarettes! Bloody cheek! The effort level doesn't even register on the Richter Scale!

In this instance, toil matters. And the dish of the day is humble pie. Tell her you are sorry – actually enunciate the word 'sorry' in a loud, clear voice and make eye contact as you say it. Then tell her you're keen to make it up to her by cooking her dinner. Suggest she might like to go shopping, read a book or visit the gym while you plod to Waitrose to purchase the necessary. If she sulkily asks what you propose to cook, tell her it's a surprise. Then choose from our tailored-to-hissy-fit list of recipes. If – after you've sedated her with one of the following – she remains resentful, either your crime was truly heinous or she's a hard woman. However, the probability is that as your offering melts in her mouth, her anger will melt with it. You've paid penance, you are absolved. Now that's what I call a happy ending.

All recipes serve 2.

SMOKED SALMON AND ASPARAGUS SALAD

Get off to a good start with a clever combination of two classy ingredients that taste divine together.

PREPARATION TIME: **7 MINUTES**
COOKING TIME: **3–4 MINUTES**

- 1 bunch asparagus bases, trimmed
- 2 tbsp sunflower oil
- 1 tbsp balsamic vinegar
- salt and freshly ground black pepper
- ½ tsp clear honey (*optional*)
- 4 thin strips smoked salmon
- 50g/2oz rocket or watercress

1 Bring a large frying pan of water to the boil. Add the asparagus and cook for 3–4 minutes until bright green and just tender. Drain. Add to a large bowl and mix in the oil, vinegar, seasoning and honey, if using. Rub the dressing into the asparagus with your hands.

2 Make four bundles of asparagus by wrapping a piece of salmon to hold each together. Add the rocket to the dressing and toss to coat. Place two asparagus bundles on each plate and arrange a small mound of rocket nearby. Pour the remaining dressing into a small bowl and serve with the salad.

HOW TO BE HER KITCHEN LOVE GOD

WARM PEARS WITH BLUE CHEESE AND WALNUTS

The pears and cheese combine to make an unusual but delicious savoury dish. Serve as a starter.

PREPARATION TIME: **15 MINUTES**
COOKING TIME: **20 MINUTES**

- 1 thick slice of white bread
- 15g/½ oz butter
- 1 tbsp olive oil
- ½ tbsp brown sugar
- handful fresh coriander leaves, roughly chopped
- 2 pears, peeled and sliced
- 125g/4oz blue cheese
- sea salt and freshly ground black pepper
- 1 tbsp walnuts, toasted and roughly chopped

1 Preheat the oven to 190°C/375°F/gas mark 5. Cut the bread into cubes, place on a baking tray and drizzle with a little oil. Cook for 15 minutes until crispy and golden.

2 Heat the butter and olive oil in a frying pan, add the sugar and coriander, cook for 1 minute. Add the pears and cook for a few minutes, turning frequently. Break the blue cheese into bite-sized pieces, add to the pan and cook until just beginning to melt. Spoon the pear mixture over the hot crispy bread and gently combine everything together. Season well, scatter over the toasted walnuts and serve in small bowls with forks.

WILD ROCKET AND BACON SALAD

The mix of crisp bacon, juicy prunes and wilted leaves tossed in a hot dressing make this salad sublime.

PREPARATION TIME: **5 MINUTES**
COOKING TIME: **10 MINUTES**

- 1 tbsp olive oil
- 4 rashers smoked streaky bacon, cut into small pieces
- 4 juicy prunes, roughly chopped
- 50g/2oz fresh wild rocket
- 150g/5oz bag mixed baby lettuce leaves
- 2 tsp oil (walnut is divine)
- 1 tbsp red wine vinegar
- freshly ground black pepper
- sea salt

1 Heat the olive oil in a wok or large frying pan. Sauté the bacon until crisp, add the prunes and cook for a minute. Spoon the bacon and prunes Into a serving bowl with the rocket and baby leaves. Add walnut oil to the pan with the red wine vinegar and stir to dislodge any bits of bacon. Drizzle the hot sauce over the leaves, season and toss.

COLD LOBSTER
WITH CHILLI MAYONNAISE

Serve up lobster and she'll know you're pushing the boat out. If you don't want to use raw egg in this recipe, mix the chilli with 4 tablespoons of prepared mayonnaise.

PREPARATION TIME: **8 MINUTES**

- 1 or 2 lobsters, cooked
- 1 egg
- 1 tsp red wine vinegar
- ½ tsp salt
- freshly ground black pepper
- 100ml/3½ fl oz each of extra virgin olive oil and vegetable oil
- juice of 1 lime
- 1 small green or red chilli, deseeded and finely chopped
- parsley or coriander, finely chopped, to garnish

1 Ask the fishmonger to halve and prepare the cooked lobsters, and refrigerate immediately.

2 To make the mayonnaise, put the egg in a food processor with the vinegar, salt and pepper and process for a few seconds. Then add the oils in a thin, steady stream. As the mixture begins to thicken, you can pour faster. After the oil is blended, process for a further 20 seconds, switch off the processor and scrape the mixture into a non-metallic bowl.

3 Add half the lime juice and mix well. Add more, according to taste. Then, bit by bit, add the chilli and season to taste. Cover and refrigerate.

4 To serve, place one or two lobster halves on a plate with a small bowl of the mayonnaise and garnish with finely chopped parsley or coriander.

HOW
TO
BE
HER
KITCHEN LOVE GOD

DUCK BREASTS WITH RASPBERRY VINEGAR

This sharp, glossy sauce contrasts perfectly with the richness of the meat. It's a dish that looks as impressive as it tastes.

PREPARATION TIME: **20 MINUTES**
COOKING TIME: **19–24 MINUTES**

- 2 duck breasts
- 2 tsp chopped fresh thyme
- salt and freshly ground black pepper
- 1 tbsp olive oil

For the sauce
- 2 tbsp olive oil
- 1 shallot, finely chopped
- 175g/6oz raspberries
- 2 tbsp soft light brown sugar
- 1 tbsp red wine vinegar

1 Preheat the oven to 220°C/425°F/gas mark 7. Prick the skin of the duck breasts all over with a fork. Sprinkle with thyme and season well with salt and freshly ground black pepper.

2 Heat the oil in a frying pan. Add the duck breasts, skin side down, and cook on a high heat for 5 minutes, then turn them over and cook for a further 2 minutes. Transfer to a baking sheet, arranged skin side up, and cook in the oven for 10–15 minutes, depending on how well done you like the meat.

3 Meanwhile, to prepare the sauce, heat the oil in a frying pan. Add the shallot and cook for a few minutes, until softened. Reserve a few raspberries for garnish, stir in the rest and cook for 1 minute. Using a wooden spoon, mash the raspberries to a pulp while still over the heat. Add the brown sugar and vinegar to the pan and bring to the boil, stirring to dissolve the sugar. Cook for 1 minute then pass through a sieve, pushing the fruit pulp with a wooden spoon to give a smooth sauce.

4 To serve, return the sauce to the pan and heat gently. Slice the duck and arrange on serving plates. Pool the sauce around and garnish with reserved raspberries.

HOW
TO
BE
HER
KITCHEN LOVE GOD

RED MULLET, MUSSEL AND GRILLED PEPPER RISOTTO WITH SAFFRON

This succulent seafood dish is bound to win back her heart. Get your fishmonger to fillet the mullet but ask for the bones so you can use them to make the stock.

PREPARATION TIME: 30–35 MINUTES
COOKING TIME: 45–60 MINUTES

- 1 red mullet, filleted
- 2 shallots, chopped
- 1 clove garlic, chopped
- 1 celery stalk, chopped
- 1 bay leaf
- handful of parsley stalks
- 600ml/1 pint water
- 24 mussels, scrubbed with 'beards' removed
- 2 red peppers
- 50g/2oz butter
- 175g/6oz arborio or risotto rice
- good pinch of saffron
- 150ml/5fl oz dry white wine
- salt and freshly ground black pepper
- 3 tbsp roughly chopped fresh parsley
- lemon wedges, to serve

1 Make the stock by putting the fish trimmings in a pan with one of the shallots, the garlic, celery, bay leaf, parsley and water. Bring to the boil, cover then simmer for 25–30 minutes. Strain, reserving the liquid.

2 Steam open the mussels in a pan with about 4 tablespoons of water. Cover and place over a high heat for about 3 minutes. Strain, adding the cooking juices to the prepared stock. Discard any mussels that have not opened and the shells.

3 Put the peppers under a hot grill to blacken the skins. Cool slightly, then peel. Chop the flesh and set aside.

4 Melt the butter in a medium pan. Add the remaining shallot and cook for 5 minutes to soften. Stir in the rice and crumble in the saffron. Cook, stirring for 2–3 minutes until the rice is translucent. Add the wine and cook, stirring, until the liquid is absorbed. Season.

5 Add about one third of the stock to the pan, and stir continuously for 8–10 minutes, until the stock is absorbed. Continue adding stock and cooking in this way until the rice is tender. Total cooking time is 20–30 minutes and the finished risotto should have a creamy consistency.

6 Cut the red mullet fillet into pieces and add to the pan near the end of cooking time. Stir in the mussels and red pepper, and adjust the seasoning. Sprinkle over the parsley and serve with lemon wedges.

HOW
TO
BE
HER
KITCHEN LOVE GOD

STEWED LAMB WITH CORIANDER AND TOASTED ALMONDS

Stewing meat makes it meltingly tender and also locks in all the delicious flavours. This has a warm Middle Eastern influence. Serve with rice or couscous.

PREPARATION TIME: **25 MINUTES**
COOKING TIME: **1½–2 HOURS**

- 1 tbsp olive oil
- 350g/12oz cubed lamb, leg or fillet
- ½ onion, chopped
- 1 garlic clove, chopped
- 1 tsp ground coriander
- ½ tsp ground cumin
- about 75ml/3fl oz cold water
- salt and freshly ground black pepper
- ½ tsp cornflour, mixed with ½ tbsp cold water
- 1 tbsp freshly chopped coriander
- 75ml/3fl oz thick natural yogurt
- toasted almond flakes
- freshly chopped coriander

1 Heat the oil in a large saucepan. Brown the lamb and then remove to a plate. Set aside. Add the onion and garlic to the pan and cook on a medium heat for 5 minutes, until softened. Stir in the spices and cook for a further 2 minutes.

2 Return the lamb to the pan and add the cold water until the meat is just covered. Season and bring to the boil. Cover,

lower the heat and simmer for 1½–2 hours until the meat
is tender. Just before serving, thicken the juices with the
cornflour, mixed with a little cold water. Then stir in the
coriander and yogurt. Heat gently to avoid curdling, but
don't worry if it does.

3 Season to taste and transfer to a warmed serving dish. Serve
sprinkled with toasted almond flakes and garnish with freshly
chopped coriander.

SALADE ROSÉ

A colourful salad, this makes a delicious accompaniment to the Cold Lobster dish (see *page 140*). The ingredients can be prepared in advance and refrigerated separately before serving.

PREPARATION TIME: **20 MINUTES**

- 1 or 2 red peppers
- 1 or 2 ripe tomatoes
- 1 small head of radicchio
- 2 tbsp extra virgin olive oil
- 1 tsp balsamic vinegar
- 1 tsp red wine vinegar

1 Grill the peppers until they are soft and blackened. Leave to cool a little, then peel, halve, deseed and cut into strips. Cover and refrigerate.

2 Next, dip the tomatoes into boiling water for 10 seconds, peel, deseed, cut into strips, cover and refrigerate. Trim the radicchio, separate the leaves and rinse. Put them in a plastic bag and refrigerate.

3 Make a vinaigrette from the remaining ingredients and season to taste. To serve, tear the leaves into bite-sized pieces and spread over two plates. Then arrange the pepper and tomato on top and drizzle over the dressing.

RICH CHOCOLATE CRÈME BRÛLÉE

The heat may be off by now but don't slack with the afters. The key to success with this is to choose good-quality ingredients and to ensure that the custard mixture is very cold and the grill is very hot.

PREPARATION TIME: **5 MINUTES**
COOKING TIME: **5 MINUTES**

- 2 good-quality chocolate fudge brownies
- 200ml/7fl oz ready-made custard
  (a rich double cream version), chilled
- 125ml/4fl oz crème fraîche, chilled
- golden, unrefined caster sugar, to sprinkle

1   Preheat the grill on its highest setting. Crumble the chocolate fudge brownies into two ramekins or heatproof dishes. Mix the very chilled custard and crème fraîche together, then spoon over the brownies. Scatter a thick layer of the golden caster sugar over the top. Grill until the sugar has caramelised.

THE ULTIMATE CHOCOLATE TRUFFLES

Decadent, hand-made chocolates served with a liqueur or coffee will round off the meal nicely and you will get top marks for the effort.

MAKES ABOUT: **15 TRUFFLES**

PREPARATION TIME: **25 MINUTES (PLUS CHILLING)**

- 125g/4oz dark chocolate, made from at least 50% cocoa solids
- 150ml/5fl oz double cream
- 1½ tbsp brandy or rum or liqueur such as Cointreau or Tia Maria
- cocoa powder

For the coating
- extra cocoa powder or finely chopped toasted hazelnuts or almonds or grated chocolate – plain, milk or white

1 Break the chocolate into small pieces and put into a large bowl with the cream. Set this over a pan of simmering water until the chocolate has melted. Remove from the heat and leave to cool. To hurry this, stand the bowl in a large bowl of cold water. Stir in the brandy, rum or liqueur of your choice.

2 When the mixture is cooled and starting to set, use an electric whisk to whip until it's light and thick. Chill it, until it's solid enough to handle.

3 Sieve cocoa onto a small plate. Take spoonfuls of the truffle mixture and roll it into the cocoa. Quickly shape into balls, using your hands. Then either re-roll in cocoa powder or in one of the other suggested coatings.

HOW
TO
BE
HER

KITCHEN LOVE GOD

STRAWBERRIES AND BRAZIL NUTS WITH CHOCOLATE SAUCE

Keep plying her with chocolate and you're well on the way to making up. You can whip up the chocolate and amaretto sauce for this wicked little number, in advance.

PREPARATION TIME: **10 MINUTES**

For the sauce
- 1 small pot (142ml) double cream
- 75g/3oz soft brown sugar
- 100g/4oz plain dark chocolate
  (minimum cocoa solids content 70 per cent)
- 25g/1oz unsalted butter
- 1 tbsp amaretto liqueur

For dipping in the sauce
strawberries and Brazil nuts

1 To make the sauce, place everything but the amaretto into a pan and stir over a gentle heat for 3–4 minutes or until smooth. Remove from the heat, stir in amaretto and place in the fridge if making in advance.

2 When ready to serve, warm the sauce through for a couple of minutes, place strawberries and nuts on a platter and pour the sauce into a bowl in the middle. Simply dip the fruits and nuts into the sauce.

- Omelette with Pesto
- Beef Niçoise Salad
- Gazpacho
- Pan-steamed Salmon with Rosemary and Lemon
- Pasta alla Puttanesca
- The Ultimate Baked Potato
- Fast and Tasty Potato Fillings
- Bubble and Squeak
- Italian Deli Sandwich
- Chicken Kebabs with Olives and Lemon
- Fried Noodles with Vegetables

8

HOME
alone

Your darling is away which means you're bound to resurrect bad habits. By all means, leave your clothes sodden in the washing machine all week. Feel free to rip open your post and drop the envelopes on the hall floor. It's your prerogative to wear the same pair of boxers twice in a row and turn them inside out on the third day. If you wish to revert to adolescence, no one is going to stop you. However, on no account neglect your cooking. Evidence of other foibles can be wiped with a quick tidy, a boil wash and a short bath. Nutritional neglect cannot. Your sweetheart wants to return to a man in the peak of health! She doesn't want to come back to a pale ghost of a fellow who barely has the strength to sweep her up in a hug. So Pot Noodle is forbidden. As is any form of takeaway unless it's a jacket potato with cottage cheese and tuna – which it probably isn't.

If you eat well, you'll look good and feel better. Even if you're pining for your woman, you won't be brought down by bad mood food (high sugar, or what your mother calls, 'rubbish'). If the football's starting in 15 minutes, you may feel reluctant to start clanking pots and pans and in a weak moment your hand may creep towards the packet of Weetabix. But you can resist. These one-pan wonders are simplish, scrumptious, and good for you. Rejoice because the washing up will be minimal and anyhow, there are no witnesses should you decide to stick a solitary plate, one knife, one fork and one saucepan in the dishwasher. So start cooking. You've treated everyone you know to your culinary talents. It's only right and proper that you also treat yourself.

HOW TO BE HER KITCHEN LOVE GOD

OMELETTE WITH PESTO

A plain omelette is pepped up with some delicious Mediterranean flavouring. Serve with toast for a filling supper.

PREPARATION TIME: **5 MINUTES**
COOKING TIME: **5 MINUTES**

- 3 medium eggs
- 1½ tbsp store-bought pesto
- salt and freshly ground black pepper
- butter or extra virgin olive oil, for frying
- 1 large slice of good brown or white bread
- about 2 tsp freshly grated Parmesan cheese

1 Beat the eggs and mix in 2 teaspoons of the pesto plus a little salt and a good helping of pepper. Heat the butter or oil in a medium frying pan, preferably non-stick, until it's hot, but not sizzling. Meanwhile, start toasting the bread.

2 When the pan is hot, pour in the egg mixture. Leave for a few seconds, then lift one edge with a spatula to let the uncooked egg mixture run underneath (don't forget about your toast). When the omelette is almost cooked to your liking (approx. 2 minutes), dot the top with the remaining pesto and sprinkle over the cheese.

3 Tilt the pan and, using a spatula, slip the omelette onto a large plate and fold in half. Serve with the toast.

4 A tomato salad with a vinaigrette is the perfect accompaniment, and is quick and easy to prepare.

HOW TO BE HER KITCHEN LOVE GOD

BEEF NIÇOISE SALAD

You can make a meal out of this substantial salad that combines rare-cooked beef, boiled eggs, new potatoes, olives and crisp vegetables.

PREPARATION TIME: **20 MINUTES**
COOKING TIME: **12 MINUTES**

- 2 eggs
- 125g/4oz beef fillet,
  cut into 2.5cm/1 inch steaks
- freshly ground coarse black pepper
- 50g/2oz French beans, trimmed
- 125g/4oz cooked new potatoes
- handful of olives
- ½ mild onion, sliced
- 1 tomato, quartered
- small, crisp lettuce heart
- handful of torn parsley leaves

For the dressing
- ½ tbsp olive oil
- ½ tbsp white wine vinegar
- ½ clove garlic, crushed
- ½ tbsp wholegrain mustard
- ½ tsp honey
- salt

1 Add the eggs to a pan of boiling water and cook for 6 minutes, then cool under running cold water.

2 Season the beef steaks liberally with the coarse ground black pepper and cook under a hot grill for about 5 minutes, turning once, until well browned on the outside but still rare inside. Leave to cool. Place the French beans in a pan of boiling water and blanch for 1 minute. Refresh in cold water and drain thoroughly.

3 Slice the beef thinly and put into the salad bowl with all the remaining ingredients except the eggs. Toss lightly. Shell and quarter the eggs and arrange them on top.

4 To make the dressing, whisk all the ingredients together in a small bowl or place them all together in a screw-top jar and shake vigorously. Drizzle over the salad just before serving.

GAZPACHO

You just need a blender to create this delicious chilled soup.

PREPARATION TIME: **15 MINUTES (PLUS CHILLING TIME)**

- 300g/11oz ripe plum tomatoes, skinned and deseeded
- ¼ cucumber, peeled
- ½ red pepper, deseeded
- ½ green pepper, deseeded
- 1 garlic clove, crushed
- ¼ red onion, peeled
- 1 tbsp white wine vinegar
- 50ml/2fl oz olive oil
- 50g/2oz fresh breadcrumbs
- salt
- ½ tsp sugar
- dash of Tabasco sauce
- a little vodka (*optional*)
- 1 ice cube

1 Reserve one tomato, a small piece of cucumber and a small piece of green pepper for the garnish.

2 Place the remaining ingredients (except the vodka and ice cube) in a blender and blend to a fine consistency. Add a few drops of iced water, if you like. Transfer to a serving dish and chill.

3 Dice the reserved tomato, cucumber and pepper for garnish. When you are ready to serve, add cold water to achieve the consistency you prefer. Stir in the vodka, if using, and pour into a bowl. Add an ice cube and the garnish.

PAN-STEAMED SALMON WITH ROSEMARY AND LEMON

Even if you're on your own, you can still treat yourself to a classy dish – the herb and citrus flavouring complements the salmon.

PREPARATION TIME: **5 MINUTES**
COOKING TIME: **10 MINUTES**

- 1 salmon steak
- butter or extra virgin olive oil, for frying
- pinch of dried rosemary
- 3 tbsp dry white wine or vermouth
- salt and freshly ground pepper
- juice of ¼ lemon

1   Wipe the fish and remove any stray scales or blood. Melt the butter in a heavy frying pan with a lid. When the butter is just starting to sizzle, add the salmon, then the rosemary, the wine or vermouth and a generous dose of salt and pepper.

2   Let the fish cook for a minute or so, then cover and cook, without turning, until it is just done (5–8 minutes).

3   Pour over the lemon juice and cook for a few seconds, then transfer the salmon to a heated plate and pour over the pan juices. Serve with vinaigrette, lengthways slices of cucumber and a lemon wedge.

HOW TO BE HER KITCHEN LOVE GOD

PASTA ALLA PUTTANESCA

Full of flavour, this easy pasta dish is covered in a hot tomato sauce that combines chilli, anchovies, capers and olives.

PREPARATION TIME: **10 MINUTES**
COOKING TIME: **15 MINUTES**

- 125g/4oz pasta (any variety)
- 1 clove of garlic, finely chopped
- 1 small dried or fresh chilli, deseeded and finely chopped
- 2 or 3 anchovy fillets, coarsely chopped
- 1 or 2 tbsp extra virgin olive oil
- 200g/7oz tin of chopped plum tomatoes
- 1 tbsp capers, coarsely chopped
- 4 or 5 stoned green or black olives, halved
- small handful of fresh parsley, preferably flat-leafed, finely chopped

1 Add the pasta to a saucepan of salted, boiling water. Cook until *al dente* – cooked, but still firm to the bite – using the instructions on the packet as a guide.

2 Meanwhile, prepare the garlic, chilli and anchovies and put in a frying pan with about 1tsp of the olive oil.

2 Cook gently for around 2–3 minutes, then add the tomatoes and increase the heat to reduce the liquid. Add the capers and olives to the pan and cook for another minute.

3 Just before serving the pasta, add the remaining oil to the sauce and reheat quickly. Sprinkle over the parsley and serve with a cucumber salad.

HOW TO BE HER KITCHEN LOVE GOD

THE ULTIMATE BAKED POTATO

It may take time to cook, but you can't beat the taste of a potato baked in the oven. Bung an extra one in to use in the Bubble and Squeak recipe, if you like (see *page 165*).

PREPARATION TIME: **5 MINUTES**
COOKING TIME: **1¼ HOURS**

- baking potato, such as King Edwards or Cara, weighing about 175g/6oz
- olive oil
- coarse sea salt

1 Preheat the oven to 220°C/425°F/gas mark 7. Scrub the potato and prick the skin all over with a fork. Use your hands to rub the olive oil Into the potato skin and then sprinkle liberally with coarse sea salt. Place the potato on a baking sheet and bake for at least 1¼ hours until crisp on the outside but tender inside. Serve at once, split and buttered, topped or filled, as desired.

2 For extra flavour, you could try rubbing dried herbs, such as rosemary or thyme, onto the oiled potato skin before baking, or flavour the oil with spices such as paprika or cayenne.

HOW TO BE HER KITCHEN LOVE GOD

FAST AND TASTY POTATO FILLINGS

Crispy bacon and herb mayonnaise

1 Grill three rashers of bacon until they are crispy. Then crumble them over dollops of mayonnaise mixed with crushed garlic and chopped herbs.

Pesto potatoes

1 Scoop out the potato flesh and mix with prepared pesto. Return to the oven for about 10 minutes and serve with a simple tomato salad

Ratatouille and feta cheese

1 Split the potato in half and spoon hot ratatouille into the centre. Crumble over feta or other cheese and grill before serving.

Smoked ham and Brie

1 Place a roll of smoked ham down the centre of a split potato. Cover with slivers of Brie and grill or bake to melt.

BUBBLE AND SQUEAK

Use up any cooked vegetables with this traditional favourite, or start from scratch. It is based on a recipe by chef Martin Lam and he prefers to use the inside of a baked potato rather than mashed potato, for a drier fluffier texture.

PREPARATION TIME: **15 MINUTES**
COOKING TIME: **10 MINUTES, APPROX.**

- 15g/½ oz butter
- ½ carrot, finely diced
- ½ small leek, finely chopped
- 50g/2oz spring greens or other cabbage, finely chopped
- 150g/5oz mashed baked potato
- pinch of ground mace
- salt and freshly ground black pepper
- seasoned flour, to coat
- oil, mixed with a little butter, for frying

1 Melt half of the butter in a large, heavy frying pan. Add the carrot and leek and sauté gently for a few minutes. Then add the spring greens or cabbage and stir until all the vegetables are tender. Add this mixture to the mashed baked potato with the remaining butter and season generously with the mace, salt and pepper. Allow to cool.

2 Shape the mixture into a patty. Coat on both sides with a little seasoned flour. Cook in the oil and butter mixture, turning once until the outside is browned and crusted and the patty is hot right through.

ITALIAN DELI SANDWICH

This mega bite should be served on the biggest baguette you can find, hollowed out. These quantities will fill a sandwich 4–5 inches long.

PREPARATION TIME: **5 MINUTES**

- 25g/1oz Genoa salami
- 25g/1oz Milano salami
- 25g/1oz mortadella
- 25g/1oz capocollo or cooked ham
- 25g/1oz provolone or Emmenthal cheese
- 25g/1oz assorted pickled vegetables or vegetables in oil – peppers, artichoke hearts or mushrooms
- ½ tbsp extra virgin olive oil
- ½ tsp red wine vinegar
- ⅛ tsp dried oregano

1 Prepare the bread and lay on the filling. The meats should go on first in overlapping layers, followed by the cheese and vegetables (cut into shreds or slices).

2 Finally, drizzle on the oil and vinegar and sprinkle on the oregano. Press the top half of the bread on very firmly, then eat immediately or, better still, leave the sandwich to ripen for an hour or more.

CHICKEN KEBABS WITH OLIVES AND LEMON

A herby marinade gives the chicken extra flavour in this healthy dish.

PREPARATION TIME: **10 MINUTES (PLUS AT LEAST 1 HOUR MARINATING)**
COOKING TIME: **5 MINUTES**

- 1–2 chicken breasts, skinned
- 2 stoned green olives
- ½ tsp grated lemon rind
- ½ tsp olive oil
- 1 tbsp chopped fresh herbs, such as dill, parsley or basil
- salt and freshly ground black pepper
- ½ small yellow pepper

1 Cut the chicken breasts into bite-sized pieces and place in a shallow, non-metallic dish. Chop the olives very finely and add to the chicken with the lemon rind, olive oil, herbs and seasoning. Toss well to mix, cover and leave to marinate for a least 1 hour before cooking.

2 Cut the pepper into bite-sized squares and thread, alternating with the chicken, onto two short skewers.

3 To cook, place the skewers under a preheated, hot grill for about 5 minutes, turning them frequently, until the peppers are lightly charred and the chicken squares are cooked through.

FRIED NOODLES WITH VEGETABLES

If you really can't stay away from the noodles, then go for this dish. Add any other ingredients you fancy or whatever's in the fridge.

PREPARATION TIME: **10 MINUTES**
COOKING TIME: **10 MINUTES**

- 125g/4oz egg noodles
- 1½ tbsp vegetable oil
- ½ clove garlic, crushed
- 2.5 cm /1 inch fresh root ginger, grated
- ½ onion, chopped
- ½ red pepper, chopped
- ½ carrot, thinly sliced
- 75g/3oz shiitake or large flat mushrooms, sliced
- 50g/2oz cabbage, shredded
- ½ tbsp soy sauce
- ½ tbsp sesame oil
- 1½ tbsp salted peanuts, chopped to serve (*optional*)

1 Cook the noodles according to the manufacturer's instructions and drain.

2 Heat the vegetable oil in a large frying pan or wok. Add the garlic and ginger and cook on a medium heat for 1 minute.

Add the chopped onion and red pepper and stir-fry for 3 minutes. Add the sliced carrot and cook for 2 minutes, then add the sliced mushrooms and shredded cabbage and stir-fry for 2 more minutes, until cooked. Add the noodles to the pan and cook, tossing until heated through. Stir in the soy sauce and sesame oil, sprinkle with chopped peanuts, if using, and serve.

HOW TO BE HER KITCHEN LOVE GOD

- Italian Meringues with Strawberries and Crème Fraîche
- Gently Poached Peaches with Fresh Basil
- Cheat's Chocolate Baked Alaska
- Cheat's Chocolate Soufflé Cake
- Chocolate Truffle Dessert
- Mascarpone and Raspberry Crêpes
- Nougat and Honey Ring
- Chilled Toffee Cream with Hot Baked Banana and Mango
- Passion-fruit and Orange Fool
- Shortbread with Warm Apple Sauce and Cinnamon-scented Cream
- Chocolate Mousse Tartlets
- Raspberry Parfait with Almond Biscotti and Bitter Chocolate Sauce
- Espresso Sauce with Chocolate Ice Cream
- Banana Salad with Crushed Amaretti and Yogurt
- Grilled Blueberry and Raspberry Crumble

9. DESSERTS

He who controls the cocoa retains power. This is because women adore dessert. If a woman is full up, she adores dessert. If a woman is dieting, she adores dessert. That said, a woman will sit in a restaurant with her man and primly wave away the dessert menu. Yet, curiously, she'll display an almost violent interest in his pudding choice. She'll wrinkle her nose as he muses over the lemon torte and forcibly guide him towards a chocolatey decision. All becomes clear when his dessert arrives. He's barely lifted his fork, and she's hijacked his coffee spoon, muttered 'tiny taste' and excavated an enormous lump of cake off his plate and tipped it into her mouth. Over the next 10 minutes, she'll keep glancing at his plate and – as he cracks a hilarious joke he's been saving up – make a sudden lunge with the spoon. His wit is wasted. She'll keep lunging until the plate is scraped clean.

The moral? Force her very own dessert upon her. Don't ask, just present. She'll be putty. As she spoons the first luscious forkful into her mouth, she'll shiver with pleasure and smile like an angel. She may even flop dramatically over the table to indicate delirious surprise. She will gaze upon you as if you are a god. Exaggeration? Just try it. You'll thank me, because this dessert-fed woman is thinking, 'Jubilation, I've found a man who knows what women want.' The effects of a delicious dessert are far-reaching. Her gratitude, her awe, plus the kicking in of an almighty sugar rush, will prompt her to suggest that you dispense with the crockery and eat off each other. Breakfast, schmeakfast! Dessert is by far the most important meal of the day … it can last all night.

Most of the recipes serve 2, but there are those with larger quantities if you have guests or just want to come back for more.

ITALIAN MERINGUES WITH STRAWBERRIES AND CRÈME FRAÎCHE

The taste of sugary meringues, fresh, sweet strawberries and a clean, sharp tang of crème fraîche is heavenly.

SERVES: **2 – 4**
PREPARATION TIME: **12–15 MINUTES**
COOKING TIME: **2 HOURS, APPROX.**

- 75g/3oz caster sugar
- 2 egg whites
- fresh, ripe strawberries
- crème fraîche

1 Preheat the oven to its lowest setting (maximum 120°C/250°C/ gas mark ½). Line two baking sheets with non-stick baking parchment.

2 Put the caster sugar and egg whites in a large heatproof bowl and set over a pan of gently simmering water. With an electric whisk, beat on high speed until the mixture is thick and holds its shape. Remove from the heat and continue to whisk for 2 minutes.

3 Using two tablespoons, shape the mixture into about 12 ovals or rounds on the baking sheets, spacing them apart. Bake for around 2 hours, until the meringues are crisp and easily peeled from the baking parchment. Leave to cool completely and serve with strawberries, or other fresh fruit, and crème fraîche.

HOW TO BE HER KITCHEN LOVE GOD

GENTLY POACHED PEACHES WITH FRESH BASIL

Serve tender peaches, poached in red wine, with your favourite ice cream or sorbet.

SERVES: **2**
PREPARATION TIME: **10 MINUTES**
COOKING TIME: **10 MINUTES**

- 125ml/4fl oz water
- 125g/4oz golden caster sugar
- 250ml/9fl oz of full-bodied red wine
- 450g/1lb peaches
- ice cream or sorbet, to serve
- handful of fresh basil leaves

1 Put the water, sugar and wine into a saucepan, heat gently until the sugar has dissolved. Simmer for 5 minutes. Cut the peaches in half, peel the fruit and remove the stones. Slice the flesh into big chunks. Add the fruit to the saucepan and simmer for 10 minutes. Leave the fruit to cool in the syrup.

2 Spoon the fruit into colourful bowls or glasses, top with scoops of ice cream or sorbet and drizzle over the chilled syrup. Scatter over fresh basil leaves and serve with a chilled bottle of dessert wine.

CHEAT'S CHOCOLATE BAKED ALASKA

This uses a shop-bought cake mix to cut down on the preparation. Leave enough time for freezing, though.

SERVES: **6**
PREPARATION TIME: **15 MINUTES**
   (**PLUS 15 MINUTES COOLING AND 2 HOURS FREEZING**)
COOKING TIME: **13–15 MINUTES APPROX.**

- half a 500g/1lb 2oz box of chocolate-cake mix, Betty Crocker, if possible
- 500ml/20fl oz tub of chocolate ice cream
- 2 egg whites
- 4 tbsp caster sugar

1 Make the cake according to the instructions on the box (remember that you are halving the quantities). Use a well-greased cake tin. When cooked, leave the cake to cool for about 15 minutes, then turn out onto a wire rack. After it has cooled to room temperature, cut into six and put the pieces on a large, non-stick baking sheet.

2 Divide the ice cream into six, putting a slice on each piece of cake. Place in the freezer for 2 hours until the cake is well frozen.

3 Preheat the oven to 180°C/350°F/gas mark 4. Beat the egg whites until they form soft peaks. Add the sugar gradually and beat into a medium-stiff meringue. Put a dollop of meringue onto each cake and ice-cream portion, and bake near the top of the oven for 2 to 3 minutes, until the meringue is lightly browned. Eat at once.

HOW TO BE HER KITCHEN LOVE GOD

CHEAT'S CHOCOLATE SOUFFLÉ CAKE

This light, fluffy pudding is another great time-saver if you are busy preparing a meal for several guests.

SERVES:**8**
PREPARATION TIME: **15 MINUTES**
COOKING TIME: **20–30 MINUTES**

- half a 500g/1lb 2oz box of chocolate-cake mix, Betty Crocker if possible
- pinch of sugar
- butter, to grease ramekins
- icing sugar, to dust

1 Preheat the oven to 180°C/350°F/gas mark 4. Make the cake batter according to the instructions on the box, but with the following exception – separate the egg whites from the yolks instead of adding them whole to the mix. (Although you are using only half the packet, for this recipe you will need the number of eggs given in the instructions.) Put the yolks into the mix. In a separate bowl, add a pinch of sugar to the egg whites and beat until they form soft peaks.

2 Grease eight ramekins generously with butter. Dust the insides with a little icing sugar, shaking off the excess. When you're ready to cook, fold a spoonful of egg white into the cake mix, stir it in, then fold in the remainder quickly but evenly.

3 Divide the mixture between the ramekins, filling them to within 1.5cm (½ inch) of the top; don't be tempted to overfill. Bake at the centre of the oven for around 20 to 30 minutes, until well risen. You can undercook these slightly if you like the centre a bit gooey. Remove from the oven, dust with icing sugar and serve immediately.

CHOCOLATE TRUFFLE DESSERT

If you are both crazed chocoholics, then a slice of this sweet, sticky cake really is something to die for.

PREPARATION TIME: **30 MINUTES**
   (PLUS 15 MINUTES COOLING AND 1 HOUR CHILLING)
COOKING TIME: **35 MINUTES, APPROX.**

For the base
- 200g/7oz plain chocolate
- 150g/5oz butter
- 125g/4oz caster sugar
- 2 eggs, beaten
- 50g/2oz flour
- ½ tsp baking powder

For the cream
- 425g/15oz plain chocolate
- 425ml/15fl oz whipping cream
- 2 tbsp brandy

To decorate
- chocolate for curls
- 2 tsp cocoa or icing sugar

1 Preheat oven to 180°C/350°F/gas mark 4. Butter the inside of a 22cm (8½ inch) spring-form cake tin and line its base with a circle of greaseproof paper.

2 Break all but 25g/1oz of the chocolate into squares and put in a bowl with the butter and sugar. Place the bowl over a pan of boiling water, making sure it doesn't touch the water. Turn

off heat. When the chocolate has melted and the sugar has dissolved, blend well. Remove the bowl and mix in the eggs.

3   Chop remaining 25g/1oz chocolate into chunks. Put the flour and baking powder in a sieve, shake into the chocolate mixture and fold in, along with the chopped chunks.

4   Spoon into the baking tin, levelling with the back of a spoon, and bake in the oven for around 35 minutes. Leave for 5 minutes, then remove from the tin and allow to cool on a wire rack. Return to the tin when fully cooled.

5   To make the cream, break the chocolate into squares and melt in a bowl over a pan of boiling water. Whisk the cream until it just begins to thicken, then add melted chocolate and brandy. Whisk to mix, but not for too long. Pour over the base and smooth with a spoon. Refrigerate for at least 1 hour to firm the topping.

6   To serve, remove cake from the tin. Shave chocolate curls with a potato peeler and scatter on top. Sprinkle with cocoa and/or icing sugar and serve with single cream, if liked.

Note
This is based on a recipe from Mandy Wagstaff's *Sweet Indulgence: 100 Great Desserts*.

HOW TO BE HER KITCHEN LOVE GOD

MASCARPONE AND RASPBERRY CRÊPES

Look for delicate sweet crêpes from the bread section in supermarkets to create this treat, and serve them cold or warmed.

SERVES: **2**

PREPARATION TIME: **10 MINUTES**

- 75g/3oz white chocolate, melted
- 125g/4oz Italian mascarpone cheese
- 1 punnet raspberries
- 75ml/3fl oz whipping cream, whipped
- 2 sweet crêpes
- warm honey to drizzle (*optional*)

1 Allow the melted chocolate to cool a little then beat in the mascarpone, followed by three-quarters of the raspberries. Fold in the cream.

2 Open out the crêpes and spoon the mascarpone onto a quarter of the circle. Tightly roll up as a cone (to do this, pick up the pancake and place in a mug). Drop a few more raspberries on top. Drizzle with warm honey to serve.

HOW TO BE HER KITCHEN LOVE GOD

NOUGAT AND HONEY RING

This impressive-looking dessert combines fruit and nuts. Check, before serving, if guests are vegetarian, as gelatine is used.

SERVES: **6**

PREPARATION TIME: **20 MINUTES (PLUS SEVERAL HOURS CHILLING)**

- 50g/2oz chopped almonds
- 50g/2oz chopped hazelnuts
- 40g/1½ oz shelled pistachio nuts
- 40g/1½ oz pine kernels
- 1 sachet of gelatine
- 200g/8oz runny honey
- 250g/10oz ricotta
- 50g/2oz candied peel
- 50g/2oz glacé cherries, chopped
- 200g/8oz double cream

1 Lightly oil a 22cm (8½ inch) ring mould. Brown the chopped almonds and hazelnuts under the grill and cool. Crush the pistachio nuts and pine kernels. Dissolve the gelatine, following the instructions on the packet, and add it to the honey. Leave to cool.

2 Mash the ricotta in a bowl and add the honey and gelatine mixture, the candied peel, the chopped cherries and all the nuts. In a separate bowl, whip the cream until stiff and then fold it into the cheese mixture.

3 Pour into the ring mould, cover and chill for several hours. When ready to eat, turn it out on a plate and decorate with fresh fruit. Delicious served with a red fruit coulis.

HOW TO BE HER KITCHEN LOVE GOD

CHILLED TOFFEE CREAM WITH HOT BAKED BANANA AND MANGO

Treat dinner guests to this delicious dessert that combines a range of tastes and sensations.

SERVES: **6**
PREPARATION TIME: **10 MINUTES (PLUS OVERNIGHT CHILLING TIME)**
COOKING TIME: **15 MINUTES**

For the toffee cream
- 568ml/20fl oz double cream
- 250g tub mascarpone
- 5 Crunchie bars

For the baked fruit
- 50g/2oz butter
- 1 mango, peeled
- juice of 1 lemon or lime
- 2 tbsp dark brown sugar
- 3 large ripe bananas

1 The night before, whisk the double cream until thick. Put the mascarpone into a bowl and soften with a metal spoon, then mix together with the cream. Break the Crunchie bars into bite-sized pieces and scatter over the cream, then fold into the mixture. Divide between six large, chunky glass tumblers or bowls, leaving space at the top of each bowl for the fruit. Cover and chill for at least 12 hours, to allow the Crunchie bars to go soft and toffee-like.

2 A few hours in advance, butter a shallow baking dish. Slice
   the mango around the stone, cut the flesh into chunks and
   place into the dish. Drizzle on the lemon or lime juice and
   sprinkle over the sugar. Just before baking, peel and slice the
   bananas diagonally, place in the dish and mix with the mango.
   Dot the fruit with butter, then bake in a preheated oven at
   180°C/350°F/gas mark 5 for 15 minutes.

3 To serve, spoon the hot baked fruit over the chilled toffee
   cream and serve immediately.

PASSION-FRUIT AND ORANGE FOOL

As well as passion-fruit, you can use any fleshy fruit, such as strawberries, raspberries or bananas, for this light and frivolous little number.

SERVES: **2**
PREPARATION TIME: **15 MINUTES**

- 1 orange
- 2 passion-fruits
- 150ml/5fl oz Greek yogurt,
  fromage frais or crème fraîche
- 2 egg whites
- 50g/2oz caster sugar
- thin, crisp biscuits, to serve

1 Pare off a little rind from the orange and save it for decoration. Finely grate the rest. Halve the passion-fruits and scoop out the seeds into a bowl. Stir in the grated orange rind and the Greek yogurt, fromage frais or crème fraîche.

2 Place the egg whites in a clean bowl and whisk them until they are soft and fluffy, then add the sugar and continue whisking until the mixture is quite stiff. Gently fold this into the fruit mixture. Spoon into tall glasses, decorate with the orange rind, cut into julienne strips, and serve with thin, crisp biscuits.

SHORTBREAD WITH WARM APPLE SAUCE AND CINNAMON-SCENTED CREAM

Buy a good-quality, shop-bought shortbread to use in this quick and easy dessert.

SERVES: **2**
PREPARATION TIME: **3 MINUTES**
COOKING TIME: **7 MINUTES**

- 25g/1oz butter
- 2 juicy sweet dessert apples, peeled, cored and grated
- 50ml/2fl oz double cream
- 1 cinnamon stick
- freshly grated nutmeg
- 1 dessertspoon clear honey or maple syrup
- 1 pack good-quality shortbread
- fresh mint to garnish

1 Heat the butter in a frying pan, add the apple and cook over a medium to high heat for 5 minutes. Meanwhile, put the cream and cinnamon in a saucepan and bring to the boil. Remove from the heat, cover and leave to stand to allow the cinnamon to infuse. Turn up the heat on the apple and cook for 1 minute. Sprinkle over grated nutmeg, add the honey or syrup and warm quickly. To serve, sandwich apple sauce between shortbread and garnish with mint. Spoon cinnamon cream around the shortbread and dust with nutmeg.

CHOCOLATE MOUSSE TARTLETS

Ultra-thin filo pastry makes a great alternative to regular pasty, and needs no preparing.

SERVES: **4**
PREPARATION TIME: **20 MINUTES**
COOKING TIME: **12–15 MINUTES**

- 6 sheets filo pastry
- 50g/2oz butter, melted
- 175g/6oz plain chocolate
- 3 eggs, separated
- 2 tbsp brandy or rum
- 25g/1oz white chocolate, grated, and a few strawberries, to decorate
- icing sugar, to dust

1 Preheat the oven to 200°C/400°F/gas mark 6. Cut the pastry into 12 x 13cm (5 inch) squares. Cover with greaseproof paper and a damp cloth. Butter 4 x 10cm (4 inch) deep tartlet tins.

2 Brush the filo squares with melted butter, putting three in each tin and draping the pastry to make softly fluted cases. Place on a baking sheet and bake for 12 to 15 minutes until crisp and golden. Allow to cool then remove the cases from the tins and transfer to a wire rack.

3 For the filling, melt the plain chocolate in a clean, dry bowl over a pan of hot water. Add the egg yolks and brandy or rum

and beat well. In another bowl, whisk the egg whites until stiff, then fold into the chocolate mixture. Leave for a minute, then spoon into the cooled filo cases.

4 The tartlets can be decorated with the grated white chocolate and strawberries and dusted with icing sugar.

RASPBERRY PARFAIT WITH ALMOND BISCOTTI AND BITTER CHOCOLATE SAUCE

Impress with your very own almond flavoured biscuits that you can make a day in advance.

SERVES: **2**

PREPARATION TIME: **30 MINUTES (PLUS AT LEAST 3 HOURS FREEZING)**

COOKING TIME: **1 HOUR**

For the biscotti (MAKES ABOUT 8)
- 25g/1oz butter
- 40g/1½ oz caster sugar
- 1 small egg
- zest of 1 lemon
- ½ tbsp lemon juice
- 75g/3oz plain flour
- ½ tsp baking powder
- 25g/1oz almonds with skins on, chopped and toasted

For the parfait
- 125ml/4fl oz full-fat milk
- zest of 1 lemon
- 75g/3oz caster sugar
- 125g/4oz cream cheese
- 125g/4oz frozen raspberries

For the chocolate sauce
- 125g/4oz plain chocolate
- 2½ tbsp water

1 For the biscotti, preheat the oven to 160°C/325°F/gas mark 3. Beat the butter and sugar in a bowl until light and fluffy. Beat in the egg, zest and juice. Sift in the flour and baking powder. Fold in the almonds. Mould the dough into a sausage ½ inch thick, 1½ inches wide, and about 8 inches long. Bake for 35 minutes until firm and brown at the edges. Cool on a wire rack then slice diagonally into oval shapes. Return to the oven and bake for 30 minutes, turning once.

2 For the parfait, put all the ingredients except the raspberries and 1oz caster sugar in a food processor and blend until smooth. Put the mixture in an airtight container and freeze for 3 hours. Put the raspberries and remaining sugar in a saucepan and cook over a medium heat for a few minutes until soft, then purée until smooth. Take the parfait mixture out of the freezer and process until smooth. Stir in the raspberry purée. Freeze until firm.

3 For the sauce, place a bowl over a pan of simmering water. Melt the chocolate and water in the bowl until smooth and glossy.

4 To serve, remove the parfait from the freezer 5 minutes before serving and spoon parfait into glass dishes, drizzle cold chocolate sauce over the top and serve with the biscotti.

HOW TO BE HER KITCHEN LOVE GOD

ESPRESSO SAUCE WITH CHOCOLATE ICE CREAM

The sauce can be made in advance for this. Just warm it up when you are ready to serve.

SERVES: **2**
PREPARATION TIME: **10 MINUTES**
COOKING TIME: **6 MINUTES**

- 150ml/5fl oz double cream
- 100g/3½ oz plain chocolate
- 2 tsp espresso coffee, cold
- chocolate ice cream
- chocolate coffee beans

1 Put the cream, chocolate and espresso in a saucepan. Heat very gently, stirring until the chocolate has melted; about 5 minutes. Bring to the boil for 1 minute, remove from the heat. Cover with cling film or foil and put to one side.

2 Scoop the ice cream into cups, warm the sauce and pour over the ice cream. Scatter over a few chocolate coffee beans and serve.

BANANA SALAD WITH CRUSHED AMARETTI AND YOGURT

If you're having a heavy main course, or you feel a bit stuffed after all those chocolate recipes, try this healthy, yet tasty, pudding.

SERVES: **2**
PREPARATION TIME: **15 MINUTES**

- few pieces of orange peel, shredded
- 1½ tbsp sugar
- 2 tbsp water
- juice of ½ small orange
- 2 or 3 ripe bananas
- 2 Amaretti biscuits
- Greek-style or bio yogurt, to serve

1 Put the orange peel in a saucepan with the sugar and water. Heat gently, for around 3 minutes, until the sugar is dissolved. Leave to cool, then add the orange juice.

2 Slice the bananas into a bowl, add the sugar syrup, then toss and set aside. Crush the Amaretti biscuits in a food processor or with a rolling pin.

3 Scoop the banana mixture into bowls and top with the yogurt and biscuit crumbs. Serve.

HOW
TO
BE
HER
KITCHEN LOVE GOD

GRILLED BLUEBERRY AND RASPBERRY CRUMBLE

Jazz up the traditional crumble with these tangy fruits to create a tasty, colourful dessert.

SERVES: **4**
PREPARATION TIME: **10 MINUTES**
COOKING TIME: **10 MINUTES, APPROX.**

- 350g/12oz blueberries
- 225g/8oz raspberries

For the crumble topping
- 175g/6oz plain flour
- 125g/4oz butter
- 40g/1½ oz ground almonds
- 50g/2oz soft light brown sugar
- finely grated rind of ½ lemon
- Greek yogurt, crème fraîche or soured cream, to serve

1 Pick over the fruits, but do not wash, and place in a shallow baking dish. The fruit should almost fill the dish. Preheat the grill to medium high.

2 To make the crumble mixture, put the flour in a bowl and rub in the butter until the mixture resembles breadcrumbs. Stir in the almonds, sugar and lemon rind. Spoon the mixture over the fruit. Don't worry if the crumble layer is a little patchy – the dish looks attractive with the fruit showing through.

HOW
TO
BE
HER

KITCHEN LOVE GOD

3 Cook the crumble under the grill for about 10 minutes until browned and bubbling hot. Serve hot or warm with Greek yogurt, crème fraîche or soured cream.

HOW
TO
BE
HER
KITCHEN LOVE GOD

Further Reading

Now you've discovered that cooking isn't such a big mystery –
in fact it's really quite enjoyable – here are some recommended
books for you to browse through. We have included familiar
culinary experts, who will provide you with even more inspiration
to keep you in the kitchen.

Good Housekeeping Cookery Book – 50th Anniversary Edition
PUBLISHER: EBURY PRESS. RRP: £25

This updated classic cookery companion explains just about
everything you need to know from how to make a cheese sauce,
to kitchen equipment and food hygiene. What's more, it contains
over 900 recipes that have been double-tested.

Delia's How to Cook
PUBLISHER: BBC BOOKS. RRP: £16.99

This is the second part of Delia Smith's well-known cooking
guide that includes store-cupboard essentials, cooking meat and
fish, and making the most of seasonal vegetables. It features 120
new recipes.

Real Cooking
Nigel Slater
PUBLISHER: PENGUIN. RRP: £12.99

Nigel Slater is a renowned cookery writer with a great style and
enjoyable down-to-earth approach to cooking. This book is all
about getting pleasure out of cooking and his easy recipes simply
use good-quality ingredients to produce great food.

HOW TO BE HER KITCHEN LOVE GOD

The 30-minute Cook

Nigel Slater

PUBLISHER: PENGUIN. RRP: £10.99

Another Nigel Slater title, this is well worth a look to get some great ideas for what to cook up quickly after a long day at work. The recipes are inspired from countries all over the world.

How to Eat – The Pleasures and Principles of Good Food

Nigella Lawson

PUBLISHER: CHATTO & WINDUS. RRP: £15

Nigella Lawson is another respected cookery writer who also has an unfussy, down-to-earth style. In this book, she shares her passion for food and has come up with 350 uncomplicated recipes.

Leith's Cookery Bible

Prue Leith and Caroline Waldegrave

PUBLISHER: BLOOMSBURY. RRP: £30

This revised and updated edition has recipes that have been thoroughly tested by students of Leith's School of Food and Wine. It includes everything from soups and starters, and vegetable dishes to main courses, stocks and puddings.

The Naked Chef

Jamie Oliver

PUBLISHER: MICHAEL JOSEPH. RRP: £18.99

Bold flavours and fresh ingredients combine in talented young chef Jamie Oliver's recipes. He also has an unpretentious style, and steers clear of culinary jargon or long and complicated methods and techniques. Again, it's all about enjoying yourself in the kitchen.

HOW TO BE HER KITCHEN LOVE GOD

Mary Berry's Complete Cookbook

PUBLISHER: DORLING KINDERSLEY. RRP: £25

Over 1,000 timed recipes are featured in this book, as well as useful tips on subjects such as presentation, garnishes and freezing. Some methods, including how to carve a joint of meat, have step-by-step pictures.

Four Seasons Cookery Book

Margaret Costa

PUBLISHER: GRUB STREET. RRP: £12.99

Although several years old, this book still proves to be an inspiration to many, including a number of famous chefs. It is all about fresh, seasonal cooking and features themes such as Comforting Breakfasts and Proper Puddings.

Index

HOW TO BE HER KITCHEN LOVE GOD

HOW TO BE HER KITCHEN LOVE GOD

HOW TO BE HER

KITCHEN LOVE GOD

HOW
TO
BE
HER

KITCHEN LOVE GOD